"Arthur Joseph's technique is the first voice instruction I've ever had that worked! I would not hesitate to recommend Vocal Awareness to anyone who depends upon the use of their vocal chords to make a living."

Lucie Arnaz
singer and actress

"Arthur's Vocal Awareness techniques continue to help enhance my vocal stature. The orderly step-by-step exercises give me usable tools to repeatedly grow in voice, color, clarity, range and power."

Arnold Schwarzenegger
actor, businessman

"I was able to learn an incredible amount about my voice and about how to have great impact with more pleasure and less pain."

Tony Robbins
author, *Unlimited Power*

"They always say that what comes out of your mouth is who you are . . . well, Arthur is going to make it sound great and make it mean something."

Pat Riley
coach, Miami Heat

"Arthur Joseph's approach to Vocal Awareness profoundly changes the way you communicate with the world. His coaching has been invaluable to me as a professional communicator."

Jane Applegate
syndicated business columnist and broadcaster

"As a professional communicator, I would highly recommend *The Sound of the Soul* to ar   her personal presentation skills. Artl   ll make your voice heard and get yo

           k Canfield
          estselling
         ‌Chicken Soup for the Soul Series*

THE SOUND OF THE SOUL

Discovering the Power of Your Voice

ARTHUR SAMUEL JOSEPH

The Vocal Awareness Institute
Encino, California

Joseph, Arthur Samuel
    The Sound of the Soul: discovering the power of your voice/Arthur S. Joseph.
        p. cm.
    Includes bibliographical references (p.).
    ISBN 1-55874-407-X
    1. Voice culture — Exercises. I. Title.
PN4197.J67 1996
808' .5—dc20   96-22365
                                                CIP

©1996 Arthur Samuel Joseph
ISBN 1-55874-407-X

Publisher: The Vocal Awareness Institute
                 P.O. Box 261021
                 Encino, CA 91426-1021

Why am I afraid to dance, I who love music, rhythm and
   song?
Why am I afraid to live, I who love life and the living colors
   of
earth and sky and sea? Why am I afraid to believe,
I who admire commitment, sincerity and trust?

Why am I afraid of love, I who yearn to give myself in
   love?
Why am I afraid, I who am not afraid? Why must I be so
ashamed of my strength, or of my weakness?
Why must I live in a cage like a criminal, defying and
   hating,
I who love peace and friendship? Was I born without a skin,
that I must wear armor in order to touch or be touched?

Eugene O'Neill

Vision is the art of seeing things unseen.

Jonathan Swift

Whatever you do, or dream you can do,
begin it. Boldness has genius, power and
magic in it.

Goethe

Other Works by Arthur Samuel Joseph

The Sound of the Soul Audiotape available from the Vocal Awareness Institute, P.O. Box 261021, Encino, CA 91426-1021, or visit the Vocal Awareness website at http://www.vocalawareness.com.

Vocal Awareness, a five-tape audio/workbook series, available from Sounds True Audio, (800) 333-9185.

Sing Your Heart Out, a two-tape audio/workbook series available from the Vocal Awareness Institute and Sounds True Audio.

Vocal Awareness video, a 100-minute videotape with workbook, available from the Vocal Awareness Institute and Sounds True Audio.

Contents

Contents

Illustrations

Acknowledgments

To God—my Source, my Spiritual Origin, without which my life would not exist.

To my mother—my hero. Without her vision and courage, mine would not have been possible.

To Mrs. Julia Kinsel, my first voice teacher. Without her gift and insight, mine would not have manifested.

To Rebecca—my wife, my soulmate. Without her, nothing would be possible.

To my sons, Isaac and Eli. Without them, life would have less meaning and I would be less whole.

To Peggy Van Pelt, my spiritual sister and creative link.

To Miriam Reed, who came into my life at the perfect time—of course.

To Darlene Bonaparte, for her belief in the Work and her generosity of spirit in preparing and editing this revision.

To Karen Adler, Christine Belleris, Toby Berlin, Michele Brourman, Betty Buckner, Lucia Cappachione, Jolie Jones, Jade Latimer, Bob Mann, Albane Navizet, Mimi Peak, Tami Simon,

Annabelle Stevens, Angelika Storm, Jim and Nancy Strohecker, Milt and David Suchin, Debra Torrez, Peter Vegso, Dahlia Wilde, Susan Merrit Woo and Calvin Woo, whose belief in the work and selfless dedication made this book possible.

To my students, without whom I would not have a canvas to paint on or a palette to paint with.

To all of you—past, present, future—I humbly thank you for sharing my journey.

Introduction

The greatest fear in our culture is the fear of public speaking. It ranks ahead of death and taxes. People say to me, "I'm afraid to speak out" or "I'm afraid that I'm exposing myself."

We do so many things to change our external selves, to change how people perceive us. We struggle to lose weight, or we dress at great expense to create an image. We exercise, have a face lift, buy the right car. We do these things, but none of these cosmetic effects touch the core of our being; and trapped in that core—and in our voice—we still carry all of the internal, unchanged pain and weakness that identify us. This book will teach you how to change your identity in a *consciously aware* manner and in a way that will change the core of your being. This book will teach you how to change your voice.

Our voice is the representation and manifestation of who we are. Changing our voice changes our being at a cellular level because when we change our voice, we change our energy. We change our life!

You will want to change your life by bringing out the best in you. This book will teach you how to do that. It will enable you to be who you truly are, without fear, allowing you to *take ownership of yourself with confidence and power.*

Working with this book, you will be introduced to *Vocal Awareness*. You will learn how to be consciously aware and to integrate the mind/body/spirit trinity into every aspect of your life.

We approach Vocal Awareness—the mind/body/spirit integration and conscious awareness—through 12 basic principles, which I call Rituals. The Rituals are based on physical mechanics and moral philosophy, and the key to using them successfully is to pay attention to the details. In reading this book, don't take a single thing for granted—not a comma, not an underline or a dash. Not a word, not a phrase or a thought. In practicing the exercises, be equally sensitive to the details of your physical instrument and psychological state. *The success of this work, as in life, lies in mastering the subtleties of your individual experience.* In that subtle discovery and subsequent awareness lie your connection with your Self and your opportunity for profound change.

The physical exercises include breathing exercises, necessary for giving birth to the new you; laryngeal strengthening exercises—vocal body building, so to speak (the larynx is your voice box); relaxation exercises, which will reduce the tension of the tongue, jaw, neck and shoulders; and finally, exercises to create the mind/body/spirit connection and enhance conscious awareness.

As you begin the vocal exercises, enjoy them. Do not be afraid of *hearing yourself* and of *expressing yourself.* It's your voice and your expression. *No judgement is allowed here!* Even if you don't like what you hear, do the exercises. As you work regularly with your voice, you will discover the strengths of your voice—and its weaknesses. But note: when I refer to weakness, I am not saying weakness is bad. Remember: no judgement. A "weakness" is only an aspect of yourself to be developed, and Vocal Awareness exercises eliminate the weakness and enhance the strengths while integrating mind/ body/spirit consciousness.

You may say you don't have time to do more exercises. Yet even one very brief Vocal Awareness exercise will literally and instantaneously change your voice and yourself. Your endorphin level will rise. You will feel better. You will be better. You will be on the path to sovereignty—to personal empowerment and ownership of yourself. This is the goal of the Vocal Awareness journey: the development of your inner power and self-esteem. You will feel so good about yourself that it will give you the confidence to go out and do what you may have been afraid to do before. And each time you complete a workout, your voice will literally and physically be stronger. *You* will literally be stronger.

To observe your work and your Self critically, yet without judgement, requires surrender to the work of conscious awareness. As you practice your exercises with consciousness and without judgement, you will learn to recognize when you are doing the exercises correctly or when you need to self-correct. You will learn to notice, for example, when your shoulders are tight and your voice strangled.

You can apply yourself as much or as little as you choose: the results are, of course, commensurate with your efforts.

Whatever your level of effort, benefit is achieved. But remember: *the key to ultimate success is conscious awareness*, which is the first step to conscious enlightenment, which leads to empowerment and to making the best choices at all times. In this way, you will have *life on your terms,* in your way.

I chose to write this book because it was needed. Books on speech therapy, singing and speaking are readily available. So, too, are books on how to put your life together, how to put your body together, how to forgive, how to forget, how to live in these high pressure times—but very few of them are comprehensive enough to affect your deepest core of being. Yet knowing how to change is absurdly simple. It's right in front of you—right inside you. It all begins with exploring your voice and the metaphor of your voice. *Because your voice is who you are.*

In this book, I will show you step by step how to do the work. Spend as little as one minute a day or as much as several hours. Depending upon the level of your desire and ambition, Vocal Awareness will change your life, and *you* will be doing the changing. Vocal Awareness can help you lose weight and feel healthy. It will help you sing better and speak better, and it can help you be happier. I know it sounds as though it's all things to all people, but that's the point I'm trying to make. *Your voice* is *all things to all people.*

I have taught Vocal Awareness in palaces and on skid row. I have taught all over the world—in Mexico and Japan, in London and Vienna, at the University of Southern California and at Yale. I have taught thousands of individuals—corporate executives and college students; movie stars such as Arnold Schwarzenegger and Anne Bancroft, Faye Dunaway and Albert

Finney; executives of Toyota/Lexus and the Walt Disney Company; sports celebrities such as Joe Namath and Pat Riley. I have taught children as young as a year and a half and adults over 100, secretaries and CEOs, beginning broadcasters and seasoned anchors, tennis stars and basketball stars, housewives and schoolteachers, therapists and doctors. They have all experienced and known success through Vocal Awareness.

I have tested and developed this work, teaching it to every age group and at every level of society. At the writing of this book, I have devoted over 32 years of my professional and artistic life to this work. Now, for the first time, I've put it on paper. I have written this book for your hand to always be in mine. Because I have taken and continue to take the journey, I know how to lead you on the Vocal Awareness path—the life path to the discovery and fulfillment of the greatest you possible!

CHAPTER 1

Opening the Window

If the eyes are the window to the soul, then Vocal Awareness opens the window and allows the sounds of the soul to soar. *Our voice represents us to the world. It is our identity.* In our voice are our joy, love and enthusiasm . . . and in our voice as well are the tension, worry and troubles of our lives. The voice reveals us completely, whether we are aware of it or not.

The human voice is both magical and mysterious. We use our voice every day, yet we know very little about it and take it for granted. Although we sense its power, more often we experience its weakness. We often wonder about our voice. Why do we speak at certain times with witty fluency and at others in a dull monotone? Why do we stutter when we're nervous? Why is our voice sometimes high and at other times low? Why do others tell us our voice is irritating? Why are we uncomfortable hearing the way we "really" sound when we listen to ourselves on a tape recorder?

This book answers these questions. It will enable you to become comfortable with your voice as you discover your natural voice, the voice that is a mirror of your inner being. (When I say "voice," I don't mean merely its auditory/vibratory aspects, but also the deeper, inner voice.) Released from tension, fears and constraints, your newly found sound will be free, effortless, expressive, conscious and fully you. In turn, you will be able to express more fully and honestly who you are. You will be able to own your voice and your power, and to *speak your truth.* By discovering, uncovering and working with your natural voice, you will learn how to *overcome all fear*—not just the fear of speaking in public or even in private, but the fear upon which all these fears are based.

This book is the definitive "how to" book. This is more than a "how to" for voice; it is an exciting and positive *"how to" for living.* You will learn how to *be who you are.* Vocal Awareness, the method for teaching this work, is a playful and loving exploration of the voice that will lead you to a world of inner development and true enlightenment.

Vocal Awareness is a new concept in vocal/life training that involves your entire being—physical, spiritual, emotional, mental. It is a challenging and enjoyable process that will bring rich reward, the opportunity *to realize your own excellence and your full potential for a bountiful and satisfying life.* Best of all, Vocal Awareness will guide you in the process of developing your greatest resource—you.

Once Upon A Time

In my favorite fairy tales and perhaps yours, too, some key magical moments transform an otherwise bleak tale of neglect or abuse, poverty or mistaken identity, into a rewarding story. My beginnings trace a similar path. Once upon a time, there was a little boy named Arthur. Arthur was a wartime "accident." He was born to a single parent named Betty. Betty was 22 when Arthur was born, and Betty worked split shifts as a practical nurse to support her young son. So until he was five, Arthur lived with his grandparents, a Jewish couple in Glendale, California.

Life was not always easy for Betty. She had known an oppressive childhood, and she struggled with both emotional scars of her upbringing as well as with many physical ailments. In spite of this, she did all she could to make Arthur's life the best possible.

Somehow Betty knew that music was important, and she started Arthur in accordion lessons when he was four years old. Arthur did not want to go to his first lesson, but his mother knew best. She took him on the street car to the accordion studio. When they got there, Arthur dug his heels into the pavement and refused to go in. His mother dragged him bodily through the door of the studio. Mr. Jack Farrigan, the genial accordion teacher, set Arthur in a chair and placed a half-sized accordion in Arthur's lap. Arthur was magically changed from a recalcitrant four-year-old into a child with a purpose. The magic had begun, and Arthur recognized that his life and destiny would be music.

Arthur studied with Mr. Farrigan for many years, until his teacher moved back to his native Canada. About that time, Arthur felt a need to sing, so he auditioned for his sixth-grade choir. He was asked to sing "America the Beautiful," but because he couldn't sing it "in tune," he was not allowed to be in the choir. So Arthur kept playing his accordion.

About this same time also, Arthur discovered anti-Semitism. It hurt when people called him "kike" or wouldn't let him be part of their group. But he had his accordion and that was still his best friend.

When he reached the seventh grade, Arthur auditioned once more for the choir. He thought he might do better now that he was in junior high. Whether he did better or not, no one recalls, but he was allowed to join Mrs. Grill's Hi-Tones. Once again, Arthur knew a magical moment. Instantly, he knew that voice would be the medium for his music and the specific direction for his life. From that day on, through high school, college and into adulthood, Arthur sang in a choir. To this day, he sometimes conducts choirs; choir is still an important part of his life. And once a year, he invites a couple of hundred people into his family home at the Hanukkah/Christmas season to lead them in holiday songs.

Much later Arthur was able to explain to himself why he loved to sing so much: he loved feeling the sound in his body. Singing felt so good; it was like an internal massage. And he was able to share how to discover this feeling with others. But I'm getting ahead of myself.

One day, when Arthur was in the eighth grade, he was sick. His mother took him to stay at his grandparents' house while she went to work. When he got there, Arthur's grandmother was bustling about the house, but his grandfather was still in bed when he should have been off to work. Arthur liked his grandfather a lot, and so he thought he would play with him to wake him up. Arthur went in and sat on his grandfather's big fat stomach and tousled his still-blond hair, but his grandfather didn't move. His grandfather was dead.

This was Arthur's first experience with death, and it became a very important part of his journey. About the same time that his grandfather died, Arthur's mother was diagnosed with pancreatitis, a painful, sometimes fatal disease. His mother was hospitalized for long periods, which left Arthur living alone. While his mother struggled for her own survival, Arthur began to learn how to struggle for his.

Arthur's mother got better, and our story moves on to high school. Music still played a very important part in Arthur's life, and even though they struggled financially, his mother never saw music as a luxury, but rather as a necessity.

When Arthur was 15, he went to his mother and said, "I want to study voice." But the lessons cost $2.00 per hour and that was more than Betty could afford on a regular basis. Arthur had been working at various jobs since he was seven years old. He had always done whatever he could to earn money, from cutting lawns to delivering newspapers to being a boxboy and busboy. So he continued working, and he helped pay for his lessons.

Magic struck when Arthur was introduced to a wonderful woman in Glendale named Julia Kinsel, and he came to another turning point in his life. Mrs. Kinsel became his first and most important voice teacher. She was a strict but fair Protestant woman, about 75 years old, who lived in a comfortable home with hundreds of books lining the walls of every room. She frequently allowed Arthur to borrow and read from her shelves, and Arthur often engaged in dialogue with her philosopher husband.

For Arthur, Mrs. Kinsel was his fairy godmother. While others saw a pudgy, insecure, confused, frightened and lonely little boy, Mrs. Kinsel saw who Arthur really was. She knew Arthur marched to a different drummer and that his gift was truly unique; she had never taught a student so gifted. Because she recognized his gifts, Mrs. Kinsel allowed Arthur, with her guidance, to conduct his own lessons. For example, in the middle of a lesson, when Arthur vocalized or sang, he often clasped his hands to his ears and shouted out, "Stop! I don't want to do it that way. I hear it this way." She helped Arthur understand that he heard vocal sound differently. For Arthur didn't just hear the pitch and the melody of the voice; he instantly felt the emotion that based it. It was as though he had "perfect pitch"—though not necessarily to recognize a B-flat when he heard one, but rather, to hear the past, present and future of a vocal sound at a deep emotional level. This rare talent was coupled with an intense desire to know how sound was made and how to keep improving it technically. Julia Kinsel's wisdom, patience, strength and freedom from dogma liberated Arthur. She opened a door that has never closed.

Arthur went off to college and majored in music, philosophy and psychology. While still in college, he became a professional entertainer. By the time he was 18, he had earned his Equity and AFTRA cards—a professional performer's union cards. He performed in musical theater, on television and in night clubs, and made some recordings, but this was not enough for him. Another voice spoke inside of him. This voice, which he kept trying to ignore, kept saying to him: "You're going to be a teacher, not just a performer."

And so at 18, he also began teaching. What an exciting experience for him! When he was teaching he sensed within himself what the sound should be like and the mechanics for producing the sound—but he didn't understand why. After a lesson he tried to figure out the "why." He read voice science books, he experimented with himself, and gradually he discovered the "whys."

Arthur discovered that he loved helping people experience singing for themselves, and he was successful doing this, just as he was successful as a performer. But in his own mind, Arthur was still the same, pudgy, frightened, lonely little boy whom Mrs. Kinsel had met years earlier.

Our story moves ahead to Arthur's 22nd year. One day, around lunch time, he was sitting in a chair on his college campus meditating. During his meditation he felt someone come up beside him. He glanced out of the corner of his eye, saw beautiful calves on a beautiful woman, and cut his meditation very short. He got up, spoke to the young lady, and because she thought she had awakened him from a nap, she apologized by offering him a bite of her candy. One thing led to another, and two nights later found them sitting in a parking lot after the dress rehearsal of a musical, kissing for the first time. With the first kiss, magic struck once more, and Arthur was reminded of a recurring dream he had since childhood of a dark girl with long black hair who looked, he realized, just like Rebecca. Arthur and Rebecca fell in love.

The next year Arthur and Rebecca were in graduate school,

married, and struggling mightily to keep their financial heads above water (together they grossed $300 a month). Arthur taught voice as well as music in Sunday school, performed around town, and did various odd jobs. By the time he was 26, the Josephs had one child, had saved to buy their first home, and were on the path to fulfilling the American dream. Then Arthur was fired from the full-time job he had for three years. Things became so bad that for a while, the Josephs were forced to use foods stamps to feed their family.

Through this experience, Arthur learned one of the seminal truths of his life. *Everything in life revolves only around two issues: to choose to do something or to choose not to do it.* He was forced to look at himself in the naked light of poverty and to choose the kind of man he was to be on the next leg of his journey, for he did not like the man he had become. He recognized that he had been using his wife as a scapegoat, telling himself that she was only intellectually supportive of his teaching Vocal Awareness full time, not emotionally supportive. This was a lie. This beautiful and pure woman was there for him 1,000 percent. But whether she was there for him 1,000 or 1 percent didn't matter because Arthur had not been there for himself. With this realization, Arthur began taking responsibility for, and ultimately ownership of, his life and his destiny. Vocal Awareness was born.

The Journey Continues

Beginning to take control of his life, Arthur placed an ad offering free introductory lessons in a local newspaper. One student called and stayed for several years. Arthur also began listening to his inner voice. One day, on a drive with his family through one of the many canyons in Los Angeles, he was aware of an interesting structure off to the right. He whizzed on past. Three miles later, he responded to his inner voice, turned around, and came back to examine a pair of enormous 20-foot high gates (the gates were actually from the set of the film *Ben Hur*). Arthur parked the car, got out, and walked through the gates into a new dimension of his life.

A lovely older woman came out to greet him and asked what he and his family were doing on her private property. She explained that the gates and grounds belonged to her and her husband, the noted American actor, Will Geer; this was their outdoor theater. She and Arthur talked, and he shared with her what he did. She mentioned that she and her family were looking for a voice teacher. Arthur began teaching the Geers. The magic had struck again.

Through the Geers, Arthur met numerous other actors, singers and performing professionals who also began studying with him. At Will Geer's 70th birthday party, Arthur met Michael Learned, who at the time played the mother on the hit TV series, *The Waltons*. She said she would like to study with him and asked for his card. A month later, Arthur hadn't heard from Michael, so he searched out her unlisted phone number and picked up the phone one Friday night at 8:00 P.M., trembling, thinking she was going to say, "Who are you and how did you get my unlisted number?" But instead Michael exclaimed, "Arthur! I'm glad you called. I lost your card, When can we begin?"

Arthur had met Ralph Waite (the father on *The Waltons*) at the same party. Ralph told him he had a theater company in Los Angeles and was looking for a teacher for the company. Arthur never heard from Ralph either, so once again, Arthur picked up the phone and called. Arthur called many times over the next several weeks, even after being told, "Don't call us, we'll call you." Finally, a meeting was set. Toward the end of this meeting, Arthur sensed (again, listening to his inner voice) that his presentation was not getting across. So he said, "Ralph, would you like to try an exercise?" Before Arthur left, a date was set to begin the program, and Arthur stayed for three years.

One day around this same time, Arthur was walking past the Mark Taper Forum in Los Angeles, one of the country's leading regional theaters. He went in and asked if the company needed what he did. "No," came the reply. He asked someone else. Again, he was told no. Arthur went home and wrote a letter to the artistic director, who wrote back saying, "Yes!" The first production that Arthur worked on at the Taper starred Tyne Daly and Eileen Brennan, who went on to become dear friends and private students. Many years later, that relationship led to Arthur becoming a professor of voice in the theater school at the University of Southern California. But more on that later.

Let's jump ahead to the age of 32. Arthur and Rebecca now had two children. They had moved into their second home and, by all accounts, life was going well. But Arthur had a fire in his belly and was not satisfied with the scope of his artistic activity. In his daily prayer and meditation sessions, he focused on fulfillment. One day the phone rang and it was a production manager for a major film company, asking if he'd like to work with Sean Connery in preparation for the movie *Annie*. Sean and Arthur began studying, but several months later, Sean pulled out of the project. Some months passed and Arthur received another phone call from another production company asking if he were available to work with Albert Finney in preparation for his role as Daddy Warbucks in the same film. Arthur and Albert worked intensely together for 18 months. When shooting began, Arthur was not invited to go to New York to work with the company on location. He made many phone calls all to no avail. But there was that inner voice again, saying, "Make one more call." So he called the line producer, who said, "Well, Arthur, submit another budget." Arthur said, "I'll pay my way to New York. I'll take no per diem. I'll stay in my cousin's apartment and I'll discount my rate."

At this point you may be thinking that Arthur prostituted himself to do this job. He gave away too much. Where was his integrity? But Arthur trusted his inner voice implicitly. Finally, he was invited to join the project on location. For the first time in their lives together, Arthur had to leave his family for a month. The separation forced him to confront being alone, the guilt of "abandoning" his family, and the feeling, in turn, of being abandoned. But Arthur wished for greater artistic and personal fulfillment, so the *risk was required* if he was going to continue his journey.

We spoke earlier of all issues in life revolving around only two things: to choose or not to choose. Confronted with this choice, Arthur and his family chose the more empowering, albeit more uncomfortable path, illustrating another Vocal Awareness paradigm: the two biggest issues we all deal with every day are (1) ownership of our power and (2) fear of abandonment. We've all been abandoned in one form or another. Why continue to do it to ourselves every day? *We all deserve to be the best of ourselves possible, but it takes real courage to own our power and face our fears.*

Back to our story. Arthur went to New York and a couple of days later met Joe Layton, the executive producer of the film. Joe was a Broadway legend. The first show Joe choreographed on Broadway, in 1957, was *The Sound of Music.* He went on to do many other musicals, films and concert tours for performers the caliber of Barbra Steisand. Joe took Arthur into a corner office, sat down with him and said, "You ruffled feathers when you arrived here, boy. Wait your turn at the end of the line. What you do doesn't count." Then Joe walked out. So now Arthur was somewhat disconsolate and bloodied— but not bowed. The next day he met Aileen Quinn, who played Annie in the film, and her mother. Aileen's mother asked Arthur if he would work with Aileen. Arthur said, "Let me check with Joe." Joe said, "Welcome aboard."

They began work the following Monday. Arthur could tell how much his work was respected because he was given a half hour at lunch, between bites of a tuna fish sandwich, in which to work. Aileen was nine years old, weighed 45 pounds, and had an octave-and-a-half range. She could barely sing the highest note in "Tomorrow," the title song, and when she sang, her head shook because of her tension. On Thursday, Aileen had her first recording session. She now had a cold, a three-

and-a-half octave range, no tension, no head shaking, and with Arthur's assistance in the recording booth, she sang "Tomorrow" in one take. A couple of weeks later, Albert Finney and Arthur were at a performance of *Barnum*, a successful musical Joe Layton created for Broadway. Joe saw them in the crowded lobby and came up to Arthur and said, "You are masterful! May I study with you?" Arthur completed the film, made all the money he needed to make, received his screen credit, and Joe and Arthur became close personal friends. Aileen, too, continued to study with Arthur for many years to come.

Let's skip ahead to Arthur's early 40s. One December he was making his annual wish list. At the top of the professional column (one column for professional and one for personal wishes), he wrote down his desire to become a university professor. A few months later found him on the campus of Yale University sitting in the office of the associate dean of the drama school, perhaps the finest drama school in the nation, explaining Vocal Awareness. The presentation was pretty much falling on deaf ears. Basically, the dean was not interested. He said, however, that when Arthur next came to the East Coast to let him know and perhaps a master class could be set up. Arthur did, it was, and the class became so successful that Arthur was invited to return again and again. He was, in fact, even invited to teach the resident voice teacher the principles of Vocal Awareness.

About this same time, Arthur received a call from the acting dean of the University of Southern California School of Theatre, who said he had been speaking with Gordon Davidson. Gordon was the artistic director of the Mark Taper Forum who had originally hired Arthur so long ago. The dean told Arthur that

USC was looking for a new voice professor and asked Arthur if he would be interested. Arthur accepted the appointment and became an adjunct professor of voice at USC. His wish was fulfilled.

Refining and Defining

Throughout Arthur's life, he always strived to be the best of himself in all ways and at all times. He strove always for excellence—not perfection, but excellence. He had earlier discovered that striving to be perfect didn't allow room to grow, so excellence became his byword. He was dogged in his drive to be the best he could become and, to that end, to live life on his terms without compromising his own or his family's values. To live life with integrity and to forgive himself when he made mistakes was his approach to empowerment. He wrote a mission statement incorporating these and other important principles in his life:

◆

I want to teach my love.

I want to teach from my purest motivations.

I want to be my love and be my purest motivation.

I want to help all the people I work with to achieve their own enlightenment and to enjoy their own empowerment . . .

I want to honor this mission every day in every thing that I do and not be afraid to become all that I'm capable of becoming.

I want to forgive myself for any mistakes in the past . . .

I want to love myself, my family and God abundantly every day.

Arthur long ago discovered that taking the often perilous journey required to fulfill a life vision demands tremendous focus and a carefully organized structure. As Arthur continued refining and defining himself and his work, the two became one. Through his personal and creative journey and through the development of Vocal Awareness, Arthur changed from being a lonely, frightened and insecure young man who was a good voice teacher to become a confident man and mature, empowered master teacher. Today, Arthur rides the crest of the wave of his own personal and professional achievements. He is poised to take his work and his personal journey into the next millennium.

CHAPTER 2

The Journey

You are about to begin a remarkable journey. The goal of the journey is to discover and develop your natural voice—the voice that embodies and expresses your innermost Self. Your voice represents you to the world and tells the world everything about you—even things you don't want the world to know, for your voice reveals your fears, your tensions, anxieties and moods.

Because it can communicate so specifically the needs and desire of the Self, our voice nurtures and envelops us in a secure and meaningful way; yet at the same time, it can distance us from our true Self, even threaten and mock us. Sometimes our voice feels alien, separate, outside of us. For example, when

17

you are called upon to speak in public, you can become short of breath and your voice can seem something quite separate from 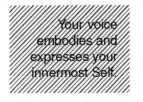 yourself. You may stammer and have trouble organizing and articulating your thoughts, your voice betraying you when you most need it. But the voice is less a dependable servant than a unique kind of mirror, displaying our Self to ourselves in enlightening, sometimes disturbing, but always honest ways.

The mirror of our voice will reveal who we *think* we are, the persona we are attempting to project. But the voice can also reveal who we *truly* are, which is what Vocal Awareness is all about. All those who work with me come to our first meeting with one voice and leave with the beginnings of another. Those who continue to work with the process and who do the Work will discover a more authentic and enriched voice, one of which they were often unaware.

As you begin this journey, you will discover the true magic and power of the voice. You will gain a mastery of the power of your own voice in your own life, and you will learn that such mastery can help you live life more fully and more successfully. You will also find that the process brings benefits more profound and far-reaching than can be imagined.

Exploring your voice will challenge and confront you, unearth hidden feelings, and awaken a fresh and enlivening sense of vulnerability and freedom—freedom to become you, freedom to awaken to and discover new choices and to make an unalterable commitment to yourself. Working with your voice will allow you the opportunity to go back to your origins, to return to that primal and embryonic experience within yourself, to the initial and primordial experience of breathing your first breath, making your first sound, expressing your first sense of Self. By reconnecting with your beginning, you can understand how you have become disconnected from your true 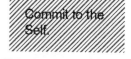 Self and your authentic voice, and *you will learn to reconnect to your Self through sound.*

Voice

At the core of every molecule in the universe is vibration. Vibration, or sound, is the very essence of all nature, that which is common to all animate and inanimate life forms. At the most infinitesimal levels, everything in the universe interconnects through vibration/sound.

The physical source of our sound—of our voice—is the larynx. It is housed within the thyroid cartilage protuberance commonly known as the Adam's apple. And yes, women have an Adam's apple. All the muscles of the body, with the exception of the larynx, are tied identically at two opposite points and function by one muscle pulling against another. The muscles of the larynx, however, are not so fixed. Instead, they lie horizontally front to back, attached to a point in the rear of the vocal tract and expanding to a "V" at the point of attachment in the front of the tract.

The vocal muscles are also the only muscles that function through air pressure. The larynx moves only as air moves through it. When we make sound, our vocal muscles shorten or lengthen, expand or contract. The velocity of the air pressure moving through the vocal folds creates the rate of vibration and pitch. Depending on the pitch, whether spoken or sung, the folds oscillate at an average rate of between 200 and 2,100 cycles per second.

Ancient Origins

Our ancestors discovered early on the power of voice and sound/vibration. Throughout recorded and unrecorded history, peoples of all cultures have sung, prayed and chanted, connecting themselves to their center within and attuning themselves to the universe through sound. The use of sound to express and experience a deep sense of atonement has continued unbroken down through the ages. To this day, people all over the world include sound in their religious and healing ceremonies and express their most profound emotions in song and chant. The rabbis, priests and monks of Judaism, Christianity, Islam, Hinduism and Buddhism all chant. Many specific examples come to mind: the shaman whose sounds send him into a mystical trance that returns him symbolically to his spiritual origins; the solitary yogi repeating the sacred "Om"; a Navajo medicine man dancing and singing in a healing ceremony; Tibetan monks chanting in unison in a remote monastery; Roman Catholic priests singing Gregorian chants; a gospel choir raising their voices in passionate praises of the Lord.

What is this magic instrument that all these mystics and religious teachers use with such expressiveness? Today, a less sacred example of that expressiveness might be rap music or other forms of pop and folk music—again, people making sound to share their story. What is it that we are all searching for or striving to communicate as we explore various expressions of sound—as we sing, chant and speak?

Our Vocal Journey Begins

Our vocal journey begins in the womb. While still in the womb, we are already exploring vocal sounds. Medical science has found that the fetus creates vocal vibrations and sound waves in its watery world, waves not unlike the sound waves created by whales and dolphins in their undersea world. The typical newborn child uses its larynx from the moment of birth, when it is thrust out of its internal aqueous environment and forced to take its first breath.

As infants, we make sounds to explore our personal universe. We do not necessarily make sounds to express what we want, but simply to express ourselves and our aliveness. We express the essence of who we are with our voice. As adults, we have adopted 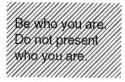 behaviors that say, "I need to *present* who I am." Through Vocal Awareness, you can relearn how to *be* who you are— just as that infant merely expresses who it is—and unlearn how not to present who you are.

What causes us to move from the being state to the presentational state? When does it begin? Let me give you an example. Let's go back to when you were six months old. You're in church, a mosque, a synagogue—some place where you are supposed to be quiet and respectful. You're going "ga ga" and "goo goo." You are being yourself. You're being held by a loved one, who pats you gently on your back and says, "Shhh." In other words, just to become socialized, just to become acculturated, just to belong to the group—before we're even consciously aware of it—we have to change. We shut down being who we are so that we can be accepted by the group—so we can be "loved" (approved of) by our parents.

Or perhaps we grew up in an angry home, where we were subjected to abuse and disapproval, where the only way we could survive was by keeping very, very quiet. Whether shushed by propriety or by anger, the effect is the same: we learn early in life to cease to sound our voice.

Daily Life

As adults we regularly encounter social situations and conflicts that do not allow for the free expression of our feelings. The resulting confusion and frustration create tension in our tongue and jaw, stifle air flow, and set up other blocks that prevent our voices from expressing ourselves fully. If we do not express our true Self, if we do not find some way to speak out, if we continue stifling our feelings when speaking with the boss or remaining polite while seething inside, we end up abusing our voice and storing the unused energy in the body as tension.

If when we speak we do not channel our energy properly— i.e., support our voice and communicate through our breath— then that energy is going to be trapped somewhere else: in the tongue, the jaw, the neck, the shoulders—or trapped in yet a worse way, possibly leading to disease or other traumas. Somewhere, somehow, the body must use that energy.

Don't get me wrong: I am not advocating rudeness and self-indulgence, but rather encouraging us to examine the "business as usual" approach to our daily communication. We may be shut down in small ways, as in the church or synagogue at six months of age—or in traumatic ways—through abuse and beatings. Regardless of the source of the original trauma, our job now is to recover our true selfhood.

The most efficient way to channel energy—in life and in communication—is through the breath. That airflow, our breath, communicates the inside of us to the outside world. We abuse our voices when we are unable to support our soundmaking with an intense and focused pressure flow and abdominal support, which is why when we scream or shout in joy or anger, we end up hoarse. Have you ever heard of a hoarse infant? No! An infant can scream and cry indefinitely. But the point is that the infant screams and cries perfectly. As adults, we must learn how to re-access our natural birthright and the ability to scream perfectly.

Our vocal folds bear the brunt of the conflict we experience in our daily lives. All of our passion, joy, confusion, struggle and pain are expressed or held within the vocal tract, the vocal passage. When we do not scream and cry perfectly, the vocal folds go into spasm, and the ligaments and membranes surrounding the larynx constrict. All the muscles in our body contract in sympathy. Too often we are unaware of this constriction, unaware of the tension throughout the body. We have grown so used to a tense body that we think it is simply the way things are. But this is not the way it has to be.

It's not unusual for me to come across an individual (such as I did recently in a workshop conducted for a Los Angeles corporation) who equates loud vocal sound with anger and aggression. Loud is, in fact, only loud. Loud carries no judgement unless we bring such to it. This individual presented himself in an extremely controlled, constrained and withdrawn manner until he was able to understand that loud was merely that—loud. He did not need to be threatened by it. The revelation changed his entire persona as well as his relationship with his co-workers.

So many similar examples come to mind. How do we express our honest, healthy and well-deserved pride in ourselves for a job well done? "Oh sweetheart, don't boast. It's not polite to brag." "Johnny and Timmy, stop that racket!" is what children hear as they play superheroes around the house, unabashedly enjoying the consummate power and freedom of their *full expression*. These admonitions and similar ones are repeated thousands of times throughout our childhood and into adulthood. Over time, we learn to shut down the natural expression of our feelings and sounds, just as my client in the corporate workshop did. Our instinctive impulse to communicate ourselves and our honest feelings to the outside world is shut down—and we don't even notice. We *settle* for it. We settle for "business as usual." Well, I want to teach you the difference between settling and accepting. I want us not to settle but to *accept* the present and learn how to work through it, and in this way to grow into our full potential.

Awareness and Consciousness

This work is called Vocal Awareness for a specific reason: because *awareness is the key.* All personal growth begins by becoming aware. Just as the corporate worker had to become aware that he was equating *loud* with *anger* before he could change his behavior, so only as we become aware can we make a difference in ourselves. *We no longer have to settle for less because we are aware that we can change.*

Consciously or unconsciously, signals and information are constantly being sent to and received by the brain. Through Vocal Awareness we can learn to identify and become aware of these ongoing messages, to become fully conscious of them, and to bring them into our heightened consciousness and knowledge. I call that *conscious awareness*.

I want to be quite sure that you are distinguishing between *awareness* and *consciousness*. The noted existential philosopher Jean Paul Sartre illustrates this distinction in his novel *Nausea*. Sartre describes a man sitting on a park bench. The man becomes aware of an image entering his peripheral vision; then the man is conscious of someone crossing in front of him and leaving his line of vision. Only after becoming *aware* of the intruder was the man able to make a *conscious decision* as to whether or not to interact with the intruder. By this same token, only after *becoming aware* that our jaw is tense can we *consciously deal* with the tension.

To be consciously aware of our Self allows the maximum use of all our options and the full integration of ourselves. No longer need you feel self-conscious; instead you will be aware of your inner voice, conscious of your Self and able to be your Self.

To become socialized and acculturated—to live in society— we have been taught, explicitly or implicitly, to stifle our natural inclinations and instincts. By the time we are adults, we believe that the way we habitually represent ourselves with our voice/ our persona is who we truly are. Such habits, however, may not have much to do with who we truly are at all. In fact, this web of socialized habits may be a mere facsimile of ourselves, based on a mythology built up over years of social conditioning as we have attempted to fit in, to belong, to be accepted in our culture. Do we have to change the very core of who we are in order to become a part of society, rather than apart from it? No! Rather, the opposite is true.

Our voice is our identity.

Heretofore, without being aware of what we were doing, we have tried to change into a Self that we think we should be. We have tried to change the core of who we are, we have done this in large measure by silencing and ignoring the inner voice and by constricting the outer voice, our outward identity. And *our voice* is exactly that: *it is our identity*. It communicates our Self to the world without our even being aware of it.

In the face of unrelenting criticism and conformity, we shut down emotionally; our entire being shuts down. Our voice becomes a mirror of this system shutdown and becomes closed, tentative, unaware, placating, defensive. We settle for our lot in life rather than recognizing and accepting our self-value. By avoiding confrontation, we believe we are protecting ourselves, when the opposite is true: we are actually placing ourselves in greater jeopardy. Shyness, tentativeness, anxiety and fear are the manifestations of shutting down our self-expression. When we learn consistently to express ourselves openly and "consciously," we become a true advocate of ourselves and discover the path to personal empowerment.

I have found in over 32 years of teaching that generally

few of us have even the slightest bit of Vocal Awareness. We are unaware of what it means to breathe freely and are unaware of the tension in our tongue, jaw, neck and shoulders. Even the best professionally trained public speakers, healers and singers have learned a "technically oriented," often superficial and disconnected approach to their art that does not address the wholeness of the person. Furthermore, the technique itself is seldom well taught.

Most people relate to technique as to a biomechanical process. Throw the ball like this, run like that, dance this way. I regard technique as being based on a trinity. Whether you are consciously aware of it or not, *technique is always the integration of mind/body/spirit.* It is never one-dimensional and never merely biomechanical. These three elements must always be integrated. *This is the trinity paradigm* that invokes all the principles of Vocal Awareness and requires being fully conscious.

All technique must integrate the mind/body/spirit consciousness.

Many of you may have had teachers, directors, coaches or others say to you, "Now you've learned how to do that, just go out and do it. Don't think about it." Imagine telling that to a tightrope walker 50 feet above the ground with no net: "Don't think about it." That is stupid advice! I want you to end, change, eradicate, completely terminate any relationship with that approach now. Instead, *think* about what you are doing/thinking *all the time*. That's what the body does. But the thinking becomes processed so rapidly that you're unaware that the body is thinking.

By heightening your conscious awareness of your thinking

body, you will be able to break the habit of unconsciousness—
and of unconscious habits. To do this, you will need to
exaggerate your behaviors. You are going to push yourself,
more or less, over the edge so that you can learn *truly* to be
aware, to be conscious, and to be you.

Through the integrative and activating techniques of Vocal
Awareness, an extraordinarily powerful and transformational
experience is achieved in an amazingly short period of time.
But you must pay attention every step of the way as you take
this journey. Notice everything: types of breath—free, tight,
short, deep; body language—free, tense; eye contact—direct,
unfocused. Emotions. Spoken language. And so much more.

If we regard attempts to access and discover the whole Self
as a mere intellectual exercise, we will never find our true Self.
The Vocal Awareness journey requires completely integrating
the sound, the breathing, the challenge, the confrontation with
our voice/ourselves, within our entire system, to force us to
expand and connect.

Vocal Awareness uses a number of paradigms. One of them,
I have discovered, is that *the true journey outward is always
and only the journey inward.* This journey allows us to give
birth to our Self by owning our own voice, bringing us the
ownership and personal sovereignty
we so deeply desire and deserve. The
key to this personal ownership is
through the metaphor of the voice.
These pages will show you how to take the journey to ownership
of your voice.

CHAPTER 3

The Naked Voice

Early in the work, I often give my students an unusual exercise. I ask them to go home, take out their tape recorders and make two recordings of their voices. For the first recording, they are asked to recite a poem and then sing a song, both of their choosing. When they make the second recording, they are asked to repeat the same poem and sing the same song, but this time without wearing their clothes.

When the tapes are brought to me for listening, I always find a difference. Usually I can tell which is which, and though I am sometimes wrong identifying which is the clothed and which is the unclothed voice, I can always identify the two different voices. Sometimes the singing voice is more on pitch; sometimes it is sweeter. Sometimes the speaking voice is more communicative, warmer, slower, or richer, but one voice—the "unclothed" voice—is always better.

The unclothed voice is the naked voice and represents the inner child, the Self that seemingly must be protected. The "clothed" voice represents the parent that is "protecting" the 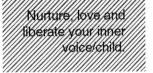 child. The parent is concerned with the outer world and its strictures; the inner child retains the essence of honesty and love for life that identifies all children. The parent is afraid to let people see the child—who we really are. But the inner child—the naked voice—betrays the unique and special selfhood that is ours, that does not need to cover itself or guard itself with defensiveness or live with fear.

Carl Jung refers to the vocal area as "the ring of fear." The clothed voice is ringed with fear. And so the presentation of our identity is ringed with fear, sometimes subtle, sometimes blatant, but always sufficient to clothe and cover our voice—our identity, our Self.

The sad fact is that we never needed to cover and hide ourselves in this way; we only assumed that we did. And so our energy goes into devising and maintaining our cover-up; out of touch with our Self, we allow others to manipulate and control us until, finally, we disempower ourselves and lose sight of our Self and our identity.

The most basic aspect of our identity is our sexuality, and our voice is closely tied to our sexuality. The voice of the male is usually lower and heavier; the voice of the female usually higher and thinner. But the connection between voice and sexuality is more than that of the sound produced. The connection is at a cellular level.

In my private work, during the first or second lesson I often show my students a slide of a larynx (Figure 3.1). I ask them what part of the anatomy they think they are seeing. Virtually every person, man or woman, identifies the slide as a picture of the cervix, or the vagina. Then I tell them that this is a slide not of the cervix, but of the larynx.

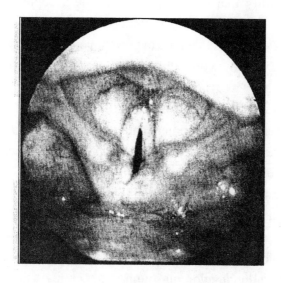

Figure 3.1
The Larynx

If you were to examine samples of tissue from both the cervix and the larynx, you would not be able to tell one from the other, for the tissues are identical. In fact, these are the only two organs in the body with identical tissue. Furthermore, if you were to examine a slide of a woman's cervix and a slide of her larynx at both 14 days and three days before the onset of menses, you would see the identical color and find the identical mucosal count, so closely are these organs interconnected.

When we speak, we open ourselves up and expose ourselves, communicating our innermost Self to the outer world. At the same time, we offer our thoughts, whether simple or profound, personal or general, to the threat of judgement. We thereby risk parental, social, public censure. There is always the possibility that our ideas may not be accepted; there is always the threat that *we* may not be accepted.

When you stand in public to present yourself, to speak your words and to show yourself and your ideas, at an unconscious level you are "wearing the emperor's new clothes." You are naked. So you cover up; you camouflage yourself.

Stop reading for a moment and look in a mirror. Open your mouth nice and wide. Notice what your tongue does: most likely it pulls back and covers your throat.

At a psychosexual level, the tongue represents a chastity belt. Just as the chastity belt locks us up and allows nothing to penetrate, so the tongue chokes back and allows nothing to escape. The tongue locks up the throat, suffocating and constricting the developing sound.

Curiously enough, the tongue is the strongest muscle per diameter in the body. Look at the diagram of the genioglossus and geniohyoid muscles which are at the base of the tongue muscle (Figure 3.2). Notice how thick and powerful they are. Equally powerful in relative terms is the temporal mandibular joint of the jaw, which is said to be capable of upwards of 6,000 pounds of pressure per square inch and which with 56 moving parts is the most complex joint in the body.

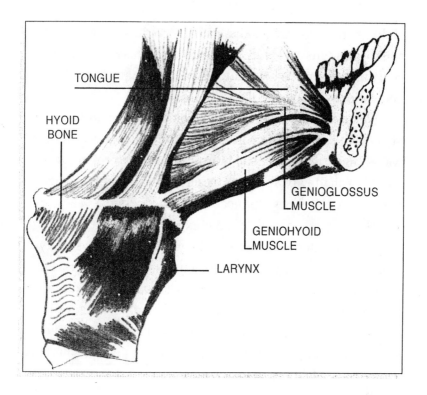

Figure 3.2
Genioglossus and Geniohyoid Muscles

This most powerful set of muscles and this most complex joint are what surround our magical vocal box, which is tied both physically and emotionally into our Self and our sexuality. Just as we may clothe the body with uncomfortable garments for the sake of fashion, so tensions in the tongue and jaw will clothe the voice for the sake of conformity.

Usually this is done unconsciously. A manner of speaking has been assumed over years and has become habit. It has been acquired from observing and imitating others—our parents, siblings, or whoever impressed us—teachers, friends, movie stars. As adults we think that we have *chosen* a manner of speaking, when in fact we have merely acquiesced through abdication.

We have accepted the clothed voice unconsciously, but we also disguise our voice consciously and deliberately, in many ways, raising our voice and lowering our voice, speaking gruffly, speaking shallowly, speaking tensely, speaking aggressively—whatever we feel best "protect" our nakedness.

The clothed voice that is our expression and that has been shaped through our contacts and conflicts with our society is equally representative of that society. It represents our values, which are too often a vestige of the warped sense of propriety that Americans have inherited from their forebears of the nineteenth century, a Victorian propriety that keeps us holding our breath and tightening our tongues and jaws because we cannot say what needs to be said.

Abuse

Statistics now coming out indicate that four out of every five females in America and one out of every five males have been emotionally or sexually abused. Both the physical stance and social behavior of the victim bear witness to such abuse. Time and again I am able to identify students who have come from abusive environments. They have weak voices, tremendous tongue and jaw tension, excessive neck and shoulder tensions, and they hold their breath in social settings—all habits developed over years of shutting themselves down to protect themselves, to keep themselves quiet and safe. Physically and emotionally they are, literally, shut down.

What is the first thing that we do when we are frightened? We hold our breath. But with Vocal Awareness, we learn to speak the truth about abuse and to speak what is not supposed to be spoken.

I had a student come to me, a woman in her late 40s, a wonderfully sensitive and caring woman who had been teaching here in Los Angeles. She showed all the signs of a sexually and/or emotionally abused individual—the weak voice, the excessive jaw tension, the avoidance of direct eye contact. When she attempted to do the early Vocal Awareness exercises—which you will be learning about shortly—and when she attempted to release tension in her jaw and to breathe freely, she went into paroxysms of anxiety and fear. As she came to trust the work, she told me her story of abuse. I also learned that she enjoyed singing, dancing and songwriting, and I encouraged her to use these outlets to support her journey of release from this burden of the past. She did, and recently she took the risk, recognized the truths about her Self and her life, and recorded a demo tape.

I am not suggesting that everyone who avoids direct eye contact or who holds excessive jaw tension has been physically or emotionally abused; but I am saying that years of traumas, minor or major, contribute directly to the lack of security we feel and express in our interactions.

As we search for the naked voice, we are able to see and speak the truth and not be embarrassed by what we discover or ashamed of what we know. We can look at ourselves as whole and complete individuals, able to show our Self with ease.

Integration/Liberation

As infants we are completely egoistic, the center of our universe. We naturally and freely express ourselves in ways that serve our needs. We cry until we are fed or changed or picked up and cuddled. We fixate on something or someone because we choose to do so. We unerringly act to provide for ourselves that which best serves our needs. It is a pity and a paradox that we have to relearn what we understood so well at birth—how to acknowledge and to provide for ourselves—and it demonstrates how important it is to confront the reality of the psychosexual relationship between voice and identity.

In the 19th century the stereotypical female was considered weak and sensitive, the stereotypical male strong and silent. These values yet permeate our vision of heroes and heroines as well as our idea of ourselves and our voice. But Vocal Awareness goes beyond stereotypes and seeks to develop what I call the androgynous voice, the balanced expression of the male and female qualities in the fulfilled individual.

A man actualizes his androgyny in part by developing his singing voice, the creed of artistic sensitivity in the voice. A woman will actualize her androgynous voice through speaking, which represents male power in our society. Through Vocal Awareness you will come to understand that there are organic and psychosexual explanations for your fear of public speaking or of communicating on your own terms. *You do not have to choose fear any longer.* You never again have to feel as though you are metaphorically prostituting yourself or being raped. You do not have to fear that you are exposing yourself.

You can make a choice not to guard your Self and not to feel vulnerable. You can make the more empowering choice to open yourself up to experience and feeling, which is the wise way of protecting yourself without guarding your Self. To be vulnerable is to be closed to who you are, but to be open allows you to be in touch with who you are.

It is a gift to be able to work on your voice because when you do so, you act as your power; you open your Self and you learn to give yourself permission to be. And this is what Vocal Awareness is about: assuring and empowering you so that you know *you have the right, without requesting permission from another, to be yourself.*

CHAPTER 4

Experiencing Sound

S ound is so powerful. *Sound is expressed emotion* and the voice is the channel through which we express that emotion and therefore ourselves.

Remember the infant, who expresses itself so freely through sound. I would like you to relate to your voice as that infant child does and allow your voice to become all that it is capable of becoming in its own time, experiencing your voice, as does the infant child, without judgement.

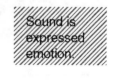
Sound is expressed emotion.

When watching the child develop, we say to ourselves, "My gosh, he sat up today," or "She rolled over!" Every seemingly insignificant new movement is a milestone. Why? Simply because it never happened before. We don't judge the rapidity of this infant's development, nor should we judge the rapidity of ours. We must, however, be critical, very clear and precise in observing the details required to fulfill ourselves, reveling in the development and growth of our voice and admiring it as we do that of our child. This critical, non-judgemental awareness allows you to journey into and out of your Self freely, within the conduit of the vocal channel, with the greatest amount of progress in the shortest amount of time.

The Breath of Life

Take a moment to begin to experience the act of expressing sound and to discover whether you are open or closed to the experience. You may find that you're embarrassed, intimidated, exhilarated, delighted or all of the above.

First, stand or sit comfortably in a chair with your back

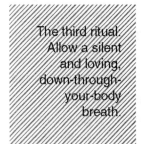

The third ritual: Allow a silent and loving, down-through-your-body breath.

straight—not tense, just comfortable. If possible, have a tape recorder available to record your comments and your sounds. The tape will also serve as a "mirror" to look into. Place your hand on your chest as you inhale. Take a deep breath with this thought:

◆

It's the top of the morning and it's great to be alive.

Notice how you feel. When you've finished, just exhale

Figure 4.1
The Breath and the Rib Cage

and relax. Now, take a different kind of breath. Gently place your hands on the sides of your rib cage and allow your body, mind and spirit to respond to this thought:

◆

Allow a silent breath.

Notice how it feels. When you've finished, exhale and relax.
Do you notice any difference?

After you have experienced this second breath, take one more step as you begin your inward journey. **Allow a silent and loving, down-through-your-body breath and allow it with consciousness and great awareness**, enjoying it while you do so.

Does that feel even more different? It does.

This is the third principle of our Vocal Awareness Ritual Checklist (I will talk more about the Vocal Awareness technique in the next chapter)—to allow a silent, loving, down-through-my-body breath and to enjoy it. Remember that to take your journey successfully requires conscious awareness at the beginning of your Vocal Awareness journey, and to breathe the Vocal Awareness way requires conscious thought. This loving breath will not happen otherwise. Taking this loving breath will become—as will all the other techniques of the checklist—more than just a simple mechanical action. It becomes a powerful, integrated, metaphorical act, a commitment that over time, leads us back to our original Self and ultimately our true destiny.

You will also notice that after a relatively brief period of time, *the body will think before the mind does,* and this new/old patterning will then be the reservoir from which you will think and act.

This is the beginning of your Vocal Awareness journey— making conscious, subtle distinctions that lead to profound change. These distinctions are not insignificant or trivial, but subtle and effective. Note what is happening inside your body when you breathe. Your "taking" breath is a clavicular action— it is upward, a vertical experience that rises into your chest. The larynx rises, the tongue flexes, and the neck and shoulders tighten. Listen to your speaking voice or singing voice afterward.

You're going to hear that it's different. It's a little higher, perhaps a little thinner, a little tighter.

Notice now how the body reacts when you allow that silent and loving, down-through-your-body breath. Notice how the intercostals, your rib cage, expand. Recall how an infant breathes. This is the way you used to breathe.

Vocal Awareness changes you rapidly because you pay attention to the use of language. Notice, for example, how the body responds differently when I say "*take* a breath" as compared with "*allow* a breath." Notice how the mind/body/spirit responded differently each time I added one more element when you took your three different breaths at the beginning of this chapter.

At this point you may also want to note the differences and the qualities of these different breaths so that you can think about them later. You might want to begin to keep a Vocal Awareness notebook to jot down your impressions of these and other experiences. You may want to note what feels most natural and most full, what feels more liberating. What feels more comfortable? Repeat this breathing ritual as often as you like to acquaint your Self with the different feelings that arise. Begin to determine how always to achieve the desired experience.

Sound

We are now going to begin to add sound to the exhalation of your breath. This sound-making is called a yawn-sigh, for it's rather like yawning and sighing at the same time. Later you can explore different kinds of sounds as you do yawn-sighs, sustaining one sound or another, opening or closing your mouth, humming, moaning, wailing or sighing—using all the vowels, *a i e o u* or *ah, ee, eh, oh, oo,* and combining them in many different ways. But right now, use one vowel sound per breath.

Make your sounds high, low, loud, happy, sad—any way you want to express yourself. Observe, however, the process of sound-making at all times. If you feel a little tickle in your throat, scratches or small irritations, they're the voice telling you, "Stop: you're hurting me a little bit. You're not doing something right." But only a few things could have gone awry. Maybe the tongue was a little tight. Let it lie comfortably against your bottom teeth doing absolutely nothing. Maybe the jaw was a little tight. Release it. Maybe the breath was too fast. Allow it to take six to eight counts and require it to be silent, slow and loving. Maybe the neck and shoulders were too tight. Let them relax. All of these are ways in which you can injure your voice by inhibiting its natural freedom. Begin to play a bit more freely with this yawn-sigh now. High, low, louder, softer, warm and rich, sweet or powerful—express yourself as consciously aware as possible in your own way, taping and listening as you go.

Here, however, is where your "inner critic" might be working overtime. Gently tell that inner critic to mind its P's and Q's and not become the judge and jury. If you want to learn to become a dancer or an athlete, you expect yourself not to be perfect all the time. You expect to look a little awkward doing it at first. Voice is the only art form that in non-visual. We begin to make sound by making sound.

> Allow/encourage your sound to come out. Allow/encourage you to come out.

What that means is that it's not going to sound so good all the time, and you'll simply have to accept that. *Allow your sound to come out.* Hear it from the perspective of the loving observer of that growing infant. Every moment, something new is being discovered.

Whenever possible, work in front of a mirror. Begin with the sound of HA as in "hat." Count to three; then begin. But first, allow a silent and loving, down-through-your-body breath. One, two, three: begin. Good. Now do that same one again, keeping your eyes on the mirror. Breathing: one, two, three. Was that one different? Notice how it feels. Notice if it feels great, notice if it doesn't. Notice how you feel. Do you like that sound or dislike it?

Let's change the vowel now to an AH as in "father." Are you ready? One, two, three: begin. Please make a note here: I don't want you to be hearing these expressions as merely sound. I want you to be feeling them as expressed emotion, i.e., a warm loving sound or a poignant sound. *Consciously connect feelings to your sound.*

Remember, too, what propels sound out of our bodies—breath. *Breath isn't only physical; it's also emotional.* It's the quickest way to open us and the quickest way to shut us down. What is the first thing that happens to the body when you're afraid, when you're in trauma? Your body holds its breath. You may pant or whatever else when you are afraid, but the first impulse is to stop breathing, to lock up the breath. Don't. Relate to the emotion of breath. Love it, accept it, enjoy and revel in it. It will create a powerful difference.

Now, allow your sound-making to become more colorful. Let it extend a little further this time, become a little bigger and perhaps more dramatic. Are you ready? Remember, don't just *take* a breath, but *allow* it. Enjoy it while doing it. One, two, three: begin. Feels pretty nifty, doesn't it? Kind of an interesting sound. Now take however long you want to do some of these exercises. Put the book down and just practice your breathing—your sound-making. When you're ready, return to the book, and we'll go a little further.

How does it feel to express sound? What are the sensations? Is it pleasant or uncomfortable, or both? Do your sounds have feelings? Do they communicate these feelings? As you continue with this journey, you will discover your natural voice—the voice that expresses and embodies the complete you. The principles and techniques you learn in Vocal Awareness will support you in your journey of self-discovery. You will find yourself using them over and over again in many different ways and applying them in practically every aspect of your life.

You will learn how to discover what I call the hub of the voice—the core of who you truly are. I always look at the hub of the voice as if it were the hub of a wheel. Various spokes that come out of that hub represent our multiple sub-personalities—the warrior, the victim, the parent, the child, the teacher, the lover. But they don't necessarily come out of a congruent voice—a balanced and integrated voice, a voice that is open and fluid, coming consistently and consciously from that hub. You are going to discover the hub of your voice and how to always tap into it and express all the various you's out of that congruent, balanced core.

As you develop your vocal muscles and the power of your voice through Vocal Awareness, you will explore all of your Self. You will experience tremendous personal growth and transformation. After just a few moments—seconds, actually—of performing the exercises, you will hear a different voice.

You will also feel and look differently. To develop the fullest of the Self, however, is the work and discipline of a lifetime.

Let's go back to our yawn. One of the simplest and most accessible ways to find your natural voice is simply to yawn. Allow the yawn to be audible, whether gently or vigorously. Pay attention to it. When the sound ends, it's where you will begin to find your "natural voice." Notice what the body does when you yawn—how it sort of stretches, like a cat awakening in the early morning sunshine. With this simple little exercise, you've begun to contact your true voice. You've begun to tap into that core voice, that hub.

Remember, Vocal Awareness is about choices and recognizing that you have options. You have the choice to ignore these options or to act on them. Remember also that *to do this work requires patience. It requires* (as I'm saying yet again) *attention to detail. It also requires form and structure.* So before making more sound, let's begin to create a way for you to do so with awareness and with consciousness.

CHAPTER 5

A Map for the Journey: The Vision and the Rituals

To take this journey with consciousness requires courage, focus and dedication. As we take the journey inward, we learn how to listen. And we learn how to speak with the outer voice the same truth and message as that of the inner voice. The more regularly we integrate the inner and outer selves, the more able we are to speak our truth and to fulfill ourselves. But fulfilling ourselves requires that we comprehend the sometimes obscure language of our dreams, direct the vision that directs our life work, and learn how to work to make the vision our reality.

Let's discuss the difference between dreams and vision. In my work, I've created a character I call the pragmatic visionary.

I've always pictured this person, man or woman, in dramatic terms—a great knight riding a huge white steed, sword and

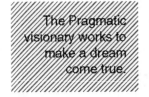

shield at the ready, prepared to do battle with the metaphorical demons we all confront on a daily basis. Like the knight's, our path is fraught with challenges, and we need a courageous figure, the alter ego that is the visionary, to help us on our way. This pragmatic visionary teaches us how to take the journey and how to ensure its success.

That's the difference between a dreamer and a pragmatic visionary. The dreamer dreams a dream, but the pragmatic visionary works to make the dream come true.

The Map

To help our pragmatic visionary and our Self on the journey, we need to know the purpose of our journey. Therefore, to take our journey, we will need a map—a Vocal Awareness map—which will make our journey easier, and a list of goals, which will give direction to our journey. Any time we don't have a clear direction, we get lost and waste time.

For example, if we wanted to drive downtown but only had a map of how to drive out of town, we would never find downtown. And if we wanted to go to another state but all we had was a map of our local community, we would never find our way out of state.

Let me give you another example. I'm hungry and go to my refrigerator. It looks like the proverbial old Mother Hubbard's cupboard—it's bare. So I put some money in my pocket, get into my car and drive to the grocery store. Part way there I realize that for whatever reason, I do not remember where the grocery store is. So I proceed a little farther down this way: It doesn't turn up. I go over that way: it's not there either. Finally I stop at a phone booth and look it up in the directory and my goodness! It was two more blocks down and to the right.

I get to the store, and I have some vague gnawing hunger inside me, but I'm not really sure what I want. My goals for coming to the store are unclear. I meander up and down the aisles, putting a little bit of this and a little bit of that in my cart, and finally I leave the grocery store, having spent more money and wasted more time than I should have. Sociologists tell us if we make a shopping list before we go to the grocery store, we save money and time. If a shopping list is good enough to buy food with, a list of goals is good enough to live my life by. *We need to be very clear about our purpose and our goals.*

We can reach a degree of clarity on these goals by writing a mission statement. *A mission statement explains our life purpose to ourselves.* It becomes a written declaration about one's reason for being. It may not be possible to write your mission statement immediately, for your reason for being may not be immediately clear. Work at defining your mission statement and then write down what you can. By writing down your ideas about your reasons for being, you begin to discover your purpose and to commit to your mission statement.

Your mission statement can change as you begin to focus on it. Most likely, it will change. It will mature. It will also become simpler and more specific. Read it regularly, until you have it completely memorized.

To support our mission statement, we must also have a goals

statement. The goals statement dictates the course our mission will take and creates the basis for the map, pointing the way. In setting our goals, we put them into a timeline based on daily, monthly and yearly structure, connecting them to the three-dimensional reality of our life and enhancing the possibility of their fruition. For example, we decide where we want to be six months from now; we then work backward on our timeline, imagining where we need to be five months from now, four months from now, and so on, to achieve what we have decided upon. We want to make our goals easily achievable, not so idealized that they are beyond our reach, but realistic and within our grasp. At the same time, we want always to keep before us, as a governing part of our mission, the highest ideals of our mission, which should be our lodestar.

We commit the steps to paper, and we commit ourselves to a daily regimen. As we go forward, working daily with all aspects of our challenge, we see better how we must work to achieve our goals. Stating your mission and setting your goals gives you a clear and focused program to follow, one that you can commit to more easily because you can visualize it and, through the writing of it, become kinesthetically involved in its creation.

By the time we reach adulthood, we've gone to school for any number of years. During that experience, we knew where we were at ten o'clock—perhaps a history class, and then at one o'clock—maybe P.E. We knew, too, how much homework to do because somebody told us to do it. But now we are adults. We are out of school, and there is no one to tell us what to do. I truly believe that *the single greatest deterrent in life to our independent success is that there is no one to tell us what to do.*

We go to school all those years, get a job, and invariably we work for somebody. Why? So someone can tell us what to do.

I want you to tell yourself what to do. Through your commitment to your mission statement and your goals, you can. It takes clarity, vision and commitment to know what to do and how to do your life's work. Because you are the only one who knows what your life work is, you are the only one who should be telling you what to do. You are responsible for fulfilling your own life goals.

Thus, with the help of our written mission statement—with the understanding of our purpose and an awareness of our goals—we can make a daily regimen part of our life and follow our map. We won't get lost. We can tell ourselves what to do and we will know how to reach our goals.

Introducing the Rituals

Now that we have set our goals and are clear about our direction (or at least have begun thinking about it), it's time to introduce the Ritual Checklist. This will structure the daily routine of our journey. I'd like you now to begin the work as I always begin it in my seminars. I'd like you to stand up and then sit down and just relax. Notice how you feel. Notice how the space in the room feels. Notice how you sat down. Did you slump in the chair? Did you cross your legs?

Now, stand up again. This time, don't just sit down and just relax. Instead, experience what it might be like simply to love and let go. Don't intellectualize it. Don't try to figure it out. Merely allow the thought of loving and letting go to filter down through the conscious mind into your muscle and sense memory.

This muscle and sense memory retains the original encoding of "loving and letting go" that is our original birthright. With that in mind, when you *choose* to do so, sit down.

Did you notice, in retrospect, that the first time—when you were "relaxing"—the body held its breath until you became more relaxed? The second time, when you were "loving and letting go," even without understanding what it meant, *the first response of the body was to breathe.* This represents empowerment. It's the body's way of saying, "Thank you for giving me permission to be me. I will inhale that permission and breathe."

Ritual #1:
Thank You to My Source

In my seminars and corporate work, after "loving and letting go" is introduced we turn to the first principle of the Ritual Checklist: *"Thank you to my source."* What does that mean? Perhaps it means a *thank you* to God. But what if you are an atheist or an agnostic and don't believe in God? Well, perhaps *"Thank you to my source"* simply means a *thank you* to your parents. But what if you say to me, "I don't like my parents. I don't want to thank them"? Let me take you to a slightly deeper understanding. Someone deserves to be thanked because someone created you. *"Thank you to my source,"* then, becomes a *thank you* to that moment of creation when you came into being. This attitude helps to develop adherence to a concept that is a significant element of this work—the concept of surrender.

Surrendering is an exceedingly important principle in Vocal

Awareness work and in the work of life. Surrendering allows us to serve the work even when, in fact, we might be afraid to take the risk that is required for our success. By allowing and requiring ourselves to do the work, by surrendering to our source and to the work, we allow and encourage ourselves to become whole. Even when we're afraid, we won't stop ourselves because we are serving something more powerful than the ego-centered Self, something bigger than merely the me. So this simple admonition, the first principle on the Vocal Awareness Ritual Checklist —thanking our source—allows us to become at all times the best of ourselves possible. It also enhances the centering and grounding aspects of the second ritual, "Loving and letting go."

Ritual #2:
Loving and Letting Go

"Loving and letting go" is a very important ritual. (Although it is the second ritual in the Vocal Awareness system, I like to introduce the Ritual Checklist with loving and letting go. This approach allows you to ease into the work and to physically experience, through the subtle use of language, specific energy shifts that occur in the mind/body/spirit relationship.) You'll notice that it separates you from one reality and puts you into another. You are more relaxed. You feel different. The space you're in feels different and sounds different. Do you notice that you feel more centered, more still? Perhaps this is a good time to begin a Vocal Awareness notebook or to jot down your impression in the notebook you've already begun.

All human sound begins, first, with an irresistible impulse

from the brain—a desire to express and communicate. As we do our work in Vocal Awareness, we focus on certain principles, certain rituals. "Loving and letting go" is one of them. As you strive to overcome fear and tension, this deceptively simple phrase will be one of your most powerful ritual tools. It will help to focus and center the mind and to create a positive, nurturing attitude. So, once again, take a moment and focus on the phrase, "Love and let go."

This phrase will hold a very personal meaning for you. "Loving" may mean experiencing your connections to your fellow beings and to loved ones. Or you may see "loving" as a spiritual acknowledgment given to one's source, to a universal power or an anthropomorphic God. For me, "loving" means giving myself permission to be the very best I can be and acknowledging the creative force that is within me. When I focus on loving, my attitude becomes open and receptive.

As we focus and think of loving, we are experiencing a feeling of acceptance and trust and a willingness to receive and share. Even if we think there is no cognitive connection, the computer of the mind will recognize one at a subconscious level, and a difference in the body consciousness will be experienced. Open to the freedom, as "letting go" releases you from everything that distracts you from your avowed purpose.

Our goal is to be free from fear, from tension, from whatever holds us back and blocks our personal progress, and growth. Remember—freedom develops out of letting go. Let go of the heavy emotional baggage you carry about with you wherever you go. Let go of tension. Let go of judgements. Accept. Don't just settle for, but *truly accept and love yourself.* Accept yourself completely as you are right now.

I look at "Loving and letting go" as one of the seminal Vocal Awareness principles. It is what I call "active meditation," something that you can integrate into your every moment as you go about your life. You can love and let go as many times in a day as you want. Try it before you walk into an important meeting. Try it before you come home from a busy day at work or before you have to say something very important to your family. Try it when you're on the telephone and you have to close a deal or make a sales pitch. Apply it any time you need to focus on being your best possible Self at that moment. That's what loving and letting go is for: to focus you in the moment, to allow you to be the best you possible right here and now. "Loving and letting go" is a dynamic phrase that can deeply affect your thinking and liberate your creative process. When we begin our work with "loving and letting go," we experience an empowering attitude that sets the tone and creates the proper atmosphere for the work that is to be done. As we let go, we become open and clear and free to do our work.

> Power develops out of freedom, freedom out of letting go, letting go out of knowledge.

Of all the techniques and principles that I have discovered over the years, "Loving and letting go" is, for me, the most helpful and most challenging. It creates amazing freedom and wakens me to extraordinary potential. Seeing so clearly, *I can surrender to my vision and my power and pursue my quest.* The permission I now have, which in truth I have always had, has often frightened and intimidated me. Through "loving and letting go," all blocks are instantly

> Surrender to your vision— become it.

removed—and that's precisely the point. I recognize that there are no blocks, and that I can have and become all I want. I discover that the fear of my own power is what has inhibited me. Through loving and letting go, I am given an opportunity to embrace myself spiritually and emotionally, simply to "let go" and leap! Each time I experience this phenomenon, I am more able to surrender to my own power. I am better able to surrender to the Divine within me, which in turn allows me to become more fully all I am capable of becoming.

For many years, I have been teaching a presentational skill class in a major corporation. About five years ago, in one of these classes, I encountered one of the most rigid and inhibited persons I have ever met. He was unable to look at the group or at me when he was speaking. His mouth was extremely tense. He could not give even a few-sentence public presentation.

At the end of a six-week course, this individual was able to describe, openly and concisely in his six-minute presentation, the trauma of his life. He spoke about the childhood experiences that had immobilized him: growing up in a strict military family, constantly moving, constantly changing schools. Finally, he shared about being five years old, being asked to speak in kindergarten and, in response, freezing up. The first time I had asked him to "Love and let go," it had terrified him. Yet even at that point, when his intellect did not accept the concept, his body did. It breathed and released its tensions and anxiety. So you see why I ask you to do the work over and over again. *The body understands before the mind does, and in this work, we develop the kinesthetic awareness of the body as intelligence.*

My student responded in spite of himself. He breathed because he was told to do so. He breathed because his unconscious mind recognized that if he were to do the work successfully, he had to surrender . Each week when he was asked to share his story, I told him to "love and let go." He found that although he tried to avoid "loving and letting go," each time I spoke the phrase, it took him to a deeper place. In the final class, he presented his story so powerfully that his classmates were crying, and at the end of his presentation, he too broke down. The class burst into spontaneous applause. He had learned how to begin loving himself, and he had learned how to begin to let go of his fear.

Sound (vibration) and breath (air) are fundamental to all life. "Loving and letting go" offers us a life of newness and aliveness.

Breathing

Vocal Awareness begins with an awareness of breath, for the breath is the source of all sound and the connective vibration of all life. Breathing is so fundamental. It is fully integrated into the historical and spiritual tapestry of our civilization. In the Old Testament (1 Kings 19:11-12), we read:

———————————————◆———————————————

And lo, the Lord passed by. There was a great and mighty wind; splitting mountains and shattering rocks by the power of the Lord; but the Lord was not in the wind. After the wind, an earthquake; but the Lord was not in the earthquake. After the earthquake, fire; but the Lord was not in the fire. And after the fire, the soft barely audible sound of almost breathing [sometimes translated a still, small voice].

———————————————————————————————

Going one step further, we note that the Hebrew name for God is frequently translated as *Yahweh*. According to Lawrence Kushner, a contemporary Jewish philosopher, "Yahweh" means the sound of breathing. The holiest name in the world, the name of the Creator, is the sound of your own breathing. In a manner of speaking then, when we breathe, it is truly as though it is the breath of God we are inhaling. How glorious to integrate mind/body/spirit energy with this conscious awareness. We know that breath can therefore be used to center us and to help us attain alignment and balance. Earlier, we introduced the ideal breathing technique, the silent and loving, down-through-your-body breath. Now we will incorporate this technique into our breathing exercises.

> By learning to be in your breath, you will learn to be in the moment. You will not anticipate the moment worrying about the outcome, but will be in the moment, and the outcome will take care of itself.

Ritual #3:
Allow a Silent, Loving,
Down-Through-My-Body Breath and Enjoy It
(Inhalation)

Stand or sit, whichever is most comfortable. Be aware of your posture. Your head is erect. Shoulders are down and released. Chest is held high, but comfortable, not rigid. Spine and upper torso are straight, but released and not tense (Figure 5.1). Allow your mouth to open in a relaxed and easy way. (This is just the beginning. Other principles for helping you to open your mouth and for enhancing the experience will be added later.)

Now release your tongue forward, letting it rest comfortably against your bottom teeth, not protruding and not tense (Figure 5.1). Allow that full, silent, loving, down-through-your-body-

Figure 5.1
The Released and Open Mouth

breath. Feel it flow through your released and open mouth, taking six to eight counts to do so.

As you breathe like this, feel the breath moving naturally down, around and through your body. Remember to loosen your neck, your shoulders, your tongue and your jaw, keeping everything in a nicely balanced position, and at all times breathing through your mouth. Some of you may know that nose breathing purifies the air. Nose breathing warms the air before it enters the trachea, but it doesn't let us get in touch with some of the other more important emotional, psychological, mechanical issues that need to be dealt with. Mouth breathing allows you to take in more air as well as to open yourself emotionally. Think of it in terms of inviting guests into your house. Breathing through your nose is like letting them in through the front door—a narrow passage that's easy to guard. Breathing through your mouth is like opening up big sliding glass doors and windows. You can't possibly guard all the entrances, and are thus more open, but are also letting in lots of fresh air. Breathing through your mouth is both mechanically and emotionally expansive and liberating.

While continuing your reading, continue breathing in this way. Deeper and deeper. Fuller and richer. All the time. When you allow yourself to breathe in this manner, you are calming the body even as you are energizing it. By paying attention to the principles of the checklist, you are continuing to refine and focus and integrate the mind/body/spirit—the trinity connection—even as *the breath helps to balance you.*

For optimum effectiveness, you will want to repeat this breathing exercise for one to two minutes. (Do it even now. Put the book down for a bit and explore and experience.) Even at the end of this short period, you will have reaped important benefits from the exercise. Once again you may also want to jot down some of those impressions in your Vocal Awareness notebook. If performed fully and consciously, you will feel centered, energized and free from tension. While breathing, it would be good to begin focusing on the nasal edge, sending your energy, without sound, up through the arc. See it soaring, releasing you and your creative energy into the universe. Keep monitoring yourself, releasing tension and enhancing your experience. Remember, too, to love and let go.

CHAPTER 6

The Workout

This is the chapter where we get to have a real "hands-on" experience with Vocal Awareness. Remember, Vocal Awareness is not just a thinking technique; it is a doing/thinking technique. This is when we really learn how to strengthen our muscles.

When Arnold Schwarzenegger first began working with me many years ago, he said to me, "My goodness, I didn't know I had a weak muscle in my body." His weak muscle, of course, was his larynx, his vocal muscle. When we first began working, I didn't want to work on his accent as much as I wanted to work on the entire voice. We made the muscle stronger. We changed the pitch of the voice, the energy of the voice, and modified the accent a bit so that it more closely fit the perceived image of the man. The voice became bolder, deeper and stronger, just as the man himself.

Now we're ready to change your voice. Here is the opportunity you've been waiting for: to change how you are perceived, *to change your reality by changing your voice.*

Ritual #4:
Release My Tongue and Jaw,
Neck and Shoulder Tension

The Tongue Release

One of the most common trouble areas for all of us is the tongue. Here is a simple technique for teaching you how to control the tension of the tongue while encouraging the freedom of the tongue. Refer to the checklist as we begin the tongue release.

Once again, stand or sit in front of a mirror so you can observe the work. Become sensitized to what it feels like to neutralize the tongue. Encourage it to lie forward, even if it is not completely comfortable for you. Encourage your tongue to simply let go and release, doing absolutely nothing. Saliva may gather in your mouth, but that's all right; the experience should be tension-free. At the same time, keep focusing on your breathing and on the principles of the checklist. We're beginning to juggle a few more balls in the air at one time. But you can do it just fine. No hurry. Does it feel interesting? Challenging? Well, let me help you further as you begin to work with the jaw release.

The Jaw Release

The most complex joint in the body is the temporal mandibular joint—that place on your face where you feel the space opening just by your ear. You may have heard of that contemporary malady called TMJ. That's the spot people are referring to. When you hear yourself or feel yourself grind your teeth or clutch your jaw, you're experiencing unresolved stress—TMJ. Pause for a moment and tighten your jaw while singing or speaking. Hear it? Feel it? Now, release your jaw tension and speak and sing again. Hear the difference? Feel it? *This is a revolutionary new exercise for eradicating TMJ and for being forever free of jaw and tongue tension.*

Let's refer now to Figure 6.1. Form a V with your hand by spreading your thumb away from your forefinger. (Note: Each

Figure 6.1
The Jaw Release

time new principles or techniques are introduced, put the book down and reflect and practice each new step for a few moments. Gradually introduce each new exercise into your routine. This will help you focus specifically and you will establish new habits and awarenesses at a very deep yet "consciously aware" level.) Rest your hand against your chin and jaw very specifically, hanging on the ledge of your chin, with your thumb on one side of your jaw and your fingers against the other. Don't squeeze with your fingers, rather balance them lightly. Allow your hand to work as a pulley, opening your mouth, releasing the tension of your tongue and jaw, neck and shoulders. Don't push or force your jaw down. Let your jaw sit in the hand. Let your hand gently and consistently pull the jaw open, striving to pull the jaw open the length of three fingers placed vertically in your

Figure 6.2
The Three-Finger Extension

mouth (begin where you comfortably can). (Figure 6.2). That's a long way, isn't it? Take the fingers out as you continue tuning into your breath, and observe in the mirror what it looks like. Note: Don't "spread" the mouth; just let it remain oval.

For a moment, I want you to experiment with different hand positions, such as putting your hand in the slightly wrong place—a bit lower on the jaw, for example—or squeezing with your fingers rather than pulling with your hand. Feel the differences. Notice it is not as secure. Find that absolute, perfectly structured, comfortable place and you'll know exactly what it's supposed to feel like. Using this gentle pressure, ease your jaw down until the mouth is open and release as comfortably as it wants to go. Remember, *let your hand pull your jaw down as you keep the jaw completely relaxed. Don't use your jaw muscles to push your jaw against your hand* (Figure 6.1). Ultimately, your mouth should be extended and released as far down as it can possibly extend, but for now, allow it to work within its limitations.

Keep releasing. Let your tongue rest easily, lightly touching your lower teeth. Periodically check in the mirror to see if you're doing all of this correctly. Keep the head erect, the neck and shoulders released. Keep your breathing moving down, around and through—and at all times, enjoy yourself. (A seeming impossibility?) Ultimately, you want a complete lack of tension in your jaw. You want to let go of any feeling of holding onto your jaw. It should be loose and hang freely. Keep your hand gently on your jaw as a reminder while you practice the breathing exercise or any of the following exercises. You may want to also experiment with what it's like when you don't put your hand there. Notice if your jaw cramps up, if it's harder to open or if tension is created. Or perhaps it's already feeling better and easier to open. Remember, *an open, released, easy mouth will keep and open, released, easy communication.* With practice, this exercise will allow you to achieve a feeling of complete release quickly and easily. Since tension depletes our energies, you will also have more energy. So as you work to release your tension, you can also look forward to this additional benefit of increased energy.

The Yawn-Sigh

In vocal training, we use both isotonic and isometric exercises to stretch and strengthen the muscles of the vocal system. Isotonic exercises are stretching exercises that cause the muscles to shorten and lengthen, the repetitive motions used in body building. Speaking is an isotonic experience because the muscles shorten and lengthen more rapidly. Isometric exercises are slow, stretching-intensive, holding exercises such as yoga, which sustain energy in the muscle for longer periods.

The principle vocal exercise used in Vocal Awareness that integrates both isotonic and isometric elements is the yawn-sigh. The yawn-sigh is a simple and excellent exercise for vocal development. Although it is primarily an isometric exercise, holding the tension constant in the muscle, it is also isotonic in that the muscle extends and contracts as pitch changes. It will integrate your inner feeling and intention with your outer expression in a simple and practical way (again, like an infant naturally expressing itself when it cries or wails). With the yawn-sigh exercise, we begin making sound. Earlier, we hummed a bit and experienced our natural, sort of undeveloped sound. Now we're going to guide the sound and allow it to emerge from our body, carried by the breath in a more directed way. This exercise will help us explore what we can do with our exhalation when we pay attention to it and guide it.

Remember that voice is energy and sound is vibration. You're now going to learn how to focus and channel that energy. This will, in time, enable you to lead, to guide, to influence others in positive ways through the power of your focus—the power of your voice in that focus. I request that you respect moral imperatives, that this work is to guide and support, not to control and conquer.

Let's begin by once again sitting in the chair or standing erect, naturally, with the checklist in front of you. You will *visualize* the emerging sound of the yawn-sigh by using the principle of the arc. As you create an arc, your entire being should focus on the task at hand. The exercise will take on the character and quality of a meditation. The more clearly and completely you are able to focus your sound and your intention into the arc, the more fully you will be experiencing and integrating the moment, once again heightening the awareness of balance. The result is that there will be no space in your thoughts for fear or self-consciousness.

Ritual #5:
Support the Sound
(by pulling my lower abdominal
muscles up and through the sound)

Ritual #6:
The Breath Precedes the Tone
(Exhalation)

The yawn-sigh is a sensual and enjoyable experience. It is like an internal massage. As your body resonates (vibrates) with sound, you will quickly discover that sound-making can be both physically and emotionally pleasurable. By doing the yawn-sigh, you will be adding two new rituals to your Vocal Awareness checklist. Number 5 becomes "Support the sound by pulling my lower abdominal muscles up and through the sound." Number 6, "The breath precedes the tone." (Don't worry if you don't understand me just yet. Stay in the moment and I'll take you there.)

> The breath precedes the tone. Support the sound by pulling your lower abdominal muscles up through the sound.

First, allow the silent and loving, down-through-your-body breath. Feel the breath moving down through your body, being aware of your balance and of releasing your tension. Feel the renewing power and energy of your breath welling up inside of you. Allow the energy to move up through your body like a geyser of water. Your thought and your energy will propel this yawn-sigh from just behind your top teeth, through the nasal edge and into a soaring/arcing sound. Put the book down and once again explore this technique.

The only way to exercise your voice is to make sound. Don't be intimidated when you make your sound. Enjoy it. Remember Eliza Doolittle in *Pygmalion* and *My Fair Lady*, and the exercise Professor Higgins gave her: " . . . Hurricanes hardly (H) ever happen." That aspirated H, that "HA," is really important to helping the sound emerge freely. It also becomes another principle of the Ritual checklist which, as I've said, is "the breath precedes the tone." Visualize the breath as a magic carpet that the sound will be riding out on. The sound will soar up through your arc and out into the universe, communicating who you are to the world at large. But it needs that "breath of God." It needs the aspirate H to precede it, to launch it. So again, just practice for a moment— "HA." (Try laughing. Hear how the H naturally precedes the sound?) Feel if your voice is stifled or stiff. Feel if it's easy—just that little "HA."

As you do your yawn-sighs, pull your lower abdominal muscles up and through your sound (Figure 6.3). Don't merely contract your stomach inward. Instead, pull it up and in. Practice this a moment before moving on. Place your hand on your stomach and feel the differences. When you pull upward, notice how the lower abdominals work more effectively? Notice also how you may have tightened your neck and shoulders as you tightened. Now focus mentally on the arc and the nasal edge, and guide the sound out of your mouth in that upward 45-degree angle that you see on page 93. "See your sound emerge, drawing itself right out through space in a continuously soaring line. I want you to see that ski jumper soaring! Put the book down and begin.

Successful? Challenging? Don't judge it, just do it again. Hand to the jaw, tongue released. Reference the checklist and use the mirror. One, loving breath, begin. If you're experiencing any throat irritation, perhaps the tongue is too tight or other parts of the body are too tense. Maybe your sound is too loud or too high or too low. The bottom line is that while you are doing yawn-sighs or any other Vocal Awareness exercise, you should never feel the

Figure 6.3
Pulling Your Abdominals up and Through the Sound

voice hurting. If it does become irritated, it is the voice's way of telling you something isn't quite right. It is saying, "Pay attention. Figure it out. Keep striving to improve." Remember, too, another bottom line is that the work should always feel joyful.

Right now, continue the exercise—*slowly, lovingly, consciously*—getting more comfortable with yourself and the experience as you go along. When you're ready, resume your reading.

Let's change the vowel sound now to a HA as in "hat" and try exploring a different pitch. Perhaps up just a little bit higher?

The actual pitch at this point doesn't matter so much. Do three in a row. Do HA, HE and HOO. At this point, do these exercises as descending scales—it can be a little trickier sometimes to ascend.

Hear your voice after having done a few yawn-sighs. It sounds different, doesn't it? Perhaps you're hearing it as more resonant, a little richer, more focused. You will always benefit from doing yawn-sighs.

Every physical action to make it more effective and efficient must include a follow-through. Whether throwing a ball or raking leaves, the body follows through its line of action. So how do we follow through with a yawn-sigh? In three ways.

1. One is biomechanically. My jaw must continue to release—it never stops. (For all singers reading this book, the distinction between "dropping your jaw" and "releasing it" will be fully developed in the chapter on singing.) As long as I hold the tone, my jaw continues to let go. When I throw that ball, I must always complete the motion. I must do the same with my jaw.

2. Whenever I throw that ball, I must throw it *through* a target, never merely at a target. The same thing happens when I make my sound. I don't want to sing *at* the note but *through* it. By the same token, when I communicate my spoken message, I don't want to speak *at* someone. I communicate *through* them. I do not broadcast to them.

3. All life is balance. Yin/yang forces are moving through our body at all times—energy/matter, cause/effect.

Balance must exist in at least two ways. In dance, for example, the dancer is always "pulling up" while mentally "releasing down" through his or her body. This enables the dancer to maintain proper balance. In voice, the energy will always move out through the arc of our voice while the emotion releases down through our body; channel your sound and soar right through the center of yourself. You've heard that old saying about "speak from your diaphragm"? That's where it comes from. I don't care for this aphorism because you don't speak from your diaphragm; you speak from your larynx and from your entire body. But I want you to feel how the diaphragm area supports your sound. The lower abdominal muscles are the fulcrum upon which your voice is balanced.

Take a moment and try doing it "wrong" (your usual way?) a couple of times—without releasing your jaw, without following through. Notice what it's like? Now when you do it a third time, guide the energy out through the arc, but don't release the emotion down through the body. The final time, put together all the principles that we have talked about and experience what it sounds like when everything is fully integrated. See that it becomes a much fuller experience in every way. It gives you something to gauge your process by, your progress, your growth. While doing your yawn-sighs, also play with volume. Do some with a full and robust voice (but remember not to shout and strain). Then also do some intimately and gently.

Remember to maintain your awareness, vocal intensity, arc, support and the other basic Vocal Awareness principles—this develops "conscious awareness." (Also, remember to play— joyfully and non-judgementally!) Remember, too, to keep the "kiss" approach in mind—"keep it simple, sweetheart." Keep the vowels and yawn-sighs simple. When you feel you've mastered the basic vowels, blend them together: HE into HAA into HA, HO into HOO, for example. Then fit them all together in any sort of random order, while keeping the focus and the mouth position the same. (The mouth, by the way, never needs to spread, even with HEY.) Once again, experiment so you recognize the difference. You can also explore the yawn-sigh by making the sound from high to low and low to high, sort of like a roller coaster. The various mouth positions will be discussed in more detail in a subsequent chapter. For now, keep it pretty basic and, above all, enjoy what you're doing.

Some people have said to me, "My goodness, I can't do these yawn-sighs in my apartment," or maybe, "I'm on the road in a hotel room. I can't do these yawn-sighs in my hotel room." There was a great football player, an all-pro linebacker by the name of Dick Butkus, who played for the Chicago Bears. Dick taught me something about doing these yawn-sighs. When he used to be a football analyst for CBS Sports, he'd be in his hotel room at 4:30 in the morning in New York, getting ready to go to the station for the broadcast. He obviously couldn't do these yawn-sighs in his hotel room too vigorously, and certainly not at 4:30 in the morning—he'd "wake the dead." So he said to himself, "Well, I need to do them. How can I best do them without disturbing anybody?" Dick's idea was to do them into a pillow. It was a very practical way to apply the exercise in an approach that would not disturb anyone. Just hold the pillow gently. Do the yawn-sighs comfortably and easily into the pillow, and you'll gain great benefit without disturbing anyone.

Now, take a few moments and just enjoy and explore the yawn-sighs. Tape yourself. Use the mirror, reference the checklist, and have a wonderful time making friends with your voice. Put the book down and when you're ready, return. How do you like the yawn-sigh? Notice its *direct impact* and the *immediate change in your voice*.

Variations

Here I want to introduce a more complex and elaborate way of doing yawn-sighs. The first way is by doing the yawn-sigh using the sound of HUNG, sustaining that NG sound in the word HUNG. It will encourage sound to resonate and vibrate more intensely in the front of the face, in the mask—the area from the tip of the top teeth to the bridge of the nose. Inside our nose we have sinus pockets that I want to send air into so the sound will resonate more intensely within the nose and behind the cheekbones. The HUNG sound is called the "Open Hum." Take a moment and try it. Remember, don't create any undue tension in the jaw or the tongue. (Even making this sound, the tip of the tongue lies loosely forward, touching the bottom teeth.)

You're going to begin to do all kinds of things you thought you were never supposed to do, such as "get real nasal." But I only want you being nasal in the ways that I tell you to because I don't want you walking around in life speaking in such a bizarre way.

An analogy might be made here once again to dance as the ballet dancer stretches his or her leg on a barre. There is absolutely nothing aesthetic about "hanging" one's leg on a barre. But the way a dancer does it is aesthetically pleasing and beautiful, and this in turn enables the body to do beautiful things in performance. There's absolutely nothing aesthetically pleasing about doing the yawn-sigh with the nasal edge, "open hum" kind of sound. But I don't want you merely to do HUNG, but rather to have a sense of awareness of your own vocal beauty as you do it. The "open hum," by the way, keeps the voice intensely locked in that very specific "mask" focus and helps to generate tremendous resonance and enhanced vibration.

Try a few exercises. Let that aspirated H out. Again, use the checklist. You should be pretty proficient at it by now. Put the book down and begin. Remember: the breath precedes the tone. Do the "open hum," see the nasal edge, the arc soaring, support and release.

Here we go again. Let me talk you through it a bit differently this time. Are you ready? Begin: breath precedes, soar, release the tongue and jaw, don't raise your head, release the neck and shoulders, support, pull the stomach up and through, have a wonderful time—and end it. Does that help?

Let's do one more just like that. Ready? One, breathing, begin. Soar, support up and through, be yourself, have a wonderful time, releasing, releasing—and finish.

After you've read through this, put the book down and try visualizing the steps before moving on. This will help integrate the "deeper listening" principle (you'll learn about this in the next chapter). Continue doing this with each new step. Read, practice, visualize, practice again and then go on. There is no hurry. Remember, you're training new habits and breaking old ones. You're engaged in a life-changing process. Allow the proper respect and take your time changing your life.

I want to stay with the yawn-sigh a bit longer. I want you to now employ it while bending from the waist. Please stand and bend over. Notice, as you do, a tendency to hold tension in the back of your neck. Let your head fall and just sort of hang limply (Figure 6.4). Get a comfortable, natural, easy feeling in your

Figure 6.4
Relaxing Your Neck and Shoulders

body and then allow yourself to stand slowly, gently, letting yourself unwind like a cat, with your head the last thing to come up. Slowly, slowly. Don't let that head lift. Let it just hang limply; don't waste tension or energy.

Let's bend over one more time now because I want you to do the yawn-sigh in this position. Gently bending from the waist, bend your knees slightly, and just let go with your upper body as completely as possible. Let your arms feel heavy—dropping toward the floor. No tension anywhere. If it's too difficult to do this while bending over, you can achieve similar results while sitting on the edge of a chair. From this position, roll your head around very gently with as much ease as possible. Allow your body to release itself in this position. Allow your body to release itself in this position while doing a yawn-sigh; there's no need to tense anywhere in your body.

Let's do one. Begin and soar from the nasal edge. Don't tense the back of your neck or tighten the shoulders. Part of the point of this is that you're displacing gravity. Come on up and rest a second, but come up slowly—don't rush, don't hurry. Relax for a moment. Take a break. When you're ready to continue again, slowly resume the same drop-over posture.

Let's try the yawn-sigh one more time. Prepare it mentally. This time I want you to do it with the "open hum," that nasal edge sound. You'll continue to see the arc soaring upward and outward. Remember, I want you to feel the energy always moving outward. Remember, I want you to feel the energy always moving out through that trajectory. Get ready with your "open hum," that NG sound in HUNG. Are you ready? Begin. Nasal edge, loving, soaring, no hurry and release.

Now we're going to do it one last time. This time I want you doing it as you arise. You're going to take a full six to eight counts to come all the way up and by the time you're fully erect, your sound will be completed. As you're arising, don't let yourself tense your neck or shoulders or anything. Keep your conscious breathing intact. I'll count you through it. Here we go: begin. Slowly, one, two, don't hurry. Loosen the neck. Four, don't raise the shoulders. Five, six, soar and release.

How does that feel? How do you feel? You'll notice your body stands straighter, taller, it's more comfortably aligned with your feet and hips. Everything just falls more naturally into place. Notice what your internal energy feels like. Feel those little tingles—that little energy rush. You will find as you work with this increased awareness that your posture will begin to correct itself naturally. You won't need to force anything. Simply notice the way you're standing or sitting and allow yourself a gentle, loving reminder. When you do a yawn-sigh from this position, you get an entirely new awareness of sound vibrating in your head and body. Remember, this variation is also an effective way to monitor yourself for tension in the neck and shoulder area, which is extremely vulnerable to stress.

Now you can sit back down as we begin to apply the hand-to-the-jaw technique, beginning to work the yawn-sigh with the jaw release. Doing the yawn-sigh this way will significantly help alleviate various jaw problems.

Form that V with your hand. Rest your hand against your chin and your jaw (Figure 6.1). Use the mirror. Remember, your chin will be the center of the V and your hand will rest on the ledge of the chin. Remember that gentle downward pressure with your hand. This is not "dropping your jaw," which locks the jaw. This is a more fluid concept that allows the jaw to move more naturally.

Let's do some yawn-sighs like this, beginning with HA as in "hat." I like using HA first because it's a very "forward" sound. Are you ready? When you are, put the book down and begin. Doesn't that feel great? It helps release any anxiety and mechanical stress by placing the hand to the jaw and makes it easier to produce sound. Do another one on the sound of HAH.

Two Fingers Under Your Tongue

Another variant of the yawn-sigh is two fingers under your tongue (Figure 6.5). This is one of my favorite exercises. It can get a little "juicy," but the benefits far outweigh the inconvenience. In placing two fingers under your tongue and letting the tongue release forward on top of your fingers, you encourage it to uncurl and release whatever tension it may be holding. No muscle. I want you to feel what it's like just to tighten your tongue and then release it so that you can become familiar with that sensation. Practice tightening and releasing, tightening and releasing.

Whenever you work with the finger-under-the-tongue

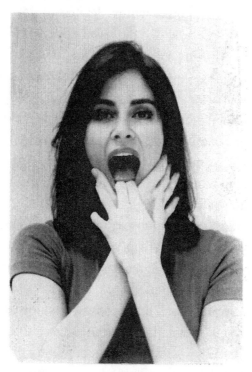

Figure 6.5
Two Fingers Under Your Tongue

exercise, the sound should always be extremely nasal. This will liberate tension in a very powerful way, and it will contribute meaningfully to a fuller and richer voice and better articulation. It enables the soft palate to rise automatically without even thinking about it. You've also created more space in the vocal tract. Making it very nasal also stresses your voice and makes it work harder—in a beneficial way. The air pressure, too, becomes more intensified.

As you do this, the tendency will be to spread your mouth and tighten things up. Don't. Just think *very nasally*. When you do this, afterward the nasality will simply translate as resonance—enhanced vibration, authority, energy, command, strength, comfort. In other words, the best of you.

Try two things now. Do the nasal edge with a very nasal sound, using two fingers. Do the second one beginning with two fingers under your tongue, then removing them while merely thinking the nasal sound without actually doing it. Listen for the enhanced resonance and character in your voice. Do you hear the benefit it creates in your speaking voice? It's a fuller, richer, warmer sound. Try it again. Remember your support: hand to the jaw, two fingers under the tongue. (It doesn't matter which hand you put where.) Keep your head erect, neck and shoulders loose (Figure 6.4). Once again, keep the checklist in full view, breath preceding the tone. Remember, maintain the focus point of the nasal edge out through the arc. On HA—begin.

Now get your fingers and hands in position again and I'll talk you through it once more. Ready? One, allowing breath: begin. Soar nasally up through the arc, pulling the stomach up and through, releasing, enjoying, soaring and expressing out and out and stop. Rest for a moment. Do another one on the sound of HAH. Hands and fingers in position. Loosen that tongue forward. Head erect. Ready? One, breathing: begin. HAH, through the arc, soaring, releasing the emotion down through the body, the energy up through the arc, the stomach pulling and balancing, shoulders and neck released—and you are through. Do a couple more now by yourself. Put the book down. When you're ready to return to the book, I'll introduce another variation.

The Tongue Pull

Before we begin this section, I want to take a moment to reinforce one of the reasons for doing these exercises and in such a specific way. Remember, sound is expressed emotion—not only sound, but breath as well. Everything we do is an expression of who we are. All the exercises are designed to help you get in touch with your Self in the fullest, most expressive way possible. Through liberating various tension areas—for example tongue tension, jaw tension—you will gain more immediate access to previously untapped and unaccessible areas of your personal expression. Also, as you do the work, I remind you to enjoy the *feeling* of it, not merely the biomechanics. You're not doing jumping jacks or push-ups. You're striving to create artful and empowered communication. Enjoy the sensuality, the creativity and the beauty of your breath and sound—your emerging voice.

I'd like you now to get a hanky or washcloth, something you can use to pull on your tongue with. Don't use a napkin or paper towel because you'll be peeling it off with your tongue.

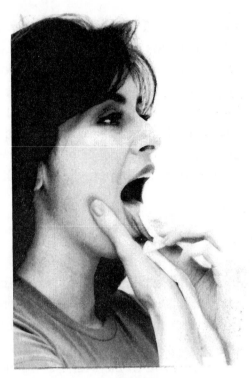

Figure 6.6
The Tongue Pull

Find something that won't stick and gently, referring to the picture in the illustration (Figure 6.6), pull your tongue down and out of your mouth. The operative word is *gently.*

This exercise will help release even more tension from the base of your tongue. It's a liberating exercise. At first you may feel that your tongue wants to fight you, but who's in charge, you or your tongue? Gently, but consistently, tell your tongue what to do by pulling it (not yanking it) downward. Keep your other hand on the jaw, helping to release its tension. Don't pull your head forward. Keep everything erect and balanced. Let's do one. Begin this one on HE. Get yourself in position, using the checklist and the mirror. Ready? One, breathing: begin. What does it feel like now? Do you hear it? Do you feel that stretching, that new energy emerging? Perhaps you will write your observations in your Vocal Awareness journal.

Do another one on the sound of HEY, as in "hey there." Remember, don't spread the mouth, don't tighten the tongue. The head is erect. One, allowing breath: begin. Nasal edge, arc, soaring, releasing, pulling, releasing and loving, expressing and through. That's really good. These yawn-sighs are so empowering, I can't even begin to tell you their value.

Do you notice the progression we're taking from the simple to the more complex? And yet, all we're doing is going HAH. It's not very complicated. With this very simple act you are changing your entire concept of communication. The effect of theses exercises at both the intrapersonal and interpersonal levels will truly amaze you.

The Pencil Technique

In my seminars, I introduce this technique by providing participants with a "magic pencil." Besides saying "Vocal Awareness," the pencil carries a very important admonition. It says, "Bite Here Gently." You have to promise that you will not do this exercise until you feel you can do it without breaking the pencil in half by biting down on it. That will create more problems than you can correct. So this exercise becomes a more advanced form of the yawn-sigh.

Listen to your voice as you do the yawn-sigh with two fingers under your tongue. Then speak directly after that. When you speak, you will immediately hear your voice sounding rich, full and resonant. Now do the yawn-sigh utilizing the pencil technique. Notice where the pencil is by looking at Figure 6.7. You'll see it's gently in front of the eye teeth. Do not spread the mouth. Do not grip the pencil in any way, merely hold it gently

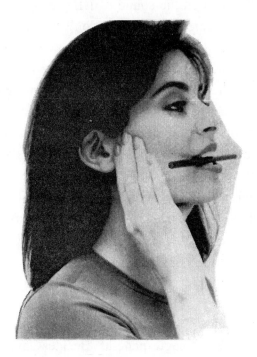

Figure 6.7
The Pencil Technique

between the teeth. (Notice the pencil is in front of the eye teeth. Do not hold it too far back in your mouth. This will enable you to direct the sound "more forward," and thus make it easier to have sharper focus and more resonance.) Try it on HA. This becomes the most extreme nasal position of the yawn-sigh.

Remove the pencil now. Do you hear the additional focus in your voice, the additional presence and clarity? It's as though your voice jumps out at you, becoming much more "forward" in its projection.

Before doing this again, let me explain the exercise in more detail. In your mind's eye, as you do the exercise, you're attempting to keep your sound "over the top of the pencil," not letting the sound drop down at any time and collapsing the soft palate as you do so. You are not forcing the sound directly out at the pencil in a horizontal trajectory, but rather keeping the sound always over the top, soaring through the arc. Practice a moment doing it the right and wrong ways—over, at and under the pencil. Do you hear and feel the differences? It doesn't matter whether the pitch is very high or very low. What does matter is that the sound always be loose and focused. Also notice, by placing your hand on your abdominals, that when you do this exercise most effectively, your stomach muscles work harder. It is a signal that you are communicating with your entire body and not working merely from "the neck up."

Are you ready to try? We'll begin on the sound of HAH as in "hat." Place the pencil gently in your mouth in front of the eye teeth. Keep your checklist at the ready. Don't spread and tighten. One, breathing: begin. Not as hard as you thought is it? Do another one, on the sound of HA. One, breathing, breath precedes the tone, and begin. Soar. Keep it in focus. Don't raise your head. Don't tighten the neck, pulling upward and through with your stomach muscles, listening and expressing—and finish. Take out the pencil. Put the book down. Do a couple of pencil exercises by yourself, perhaps even taping yourself. However you do it, practice well. When you're finished, come on back.

Remember as you do the yawn-sigh exercises not to simply do them mechanically. Do them integratively—mind/body/spirit. Remember not to go for the result. Don't try to just "hit the bull's eye." Don't compare or compete; just express and experience the exercises. Simply *be yourself. Remember to listen deeply, pay attention and enjoy.*

These yawn-sighs become a manifestation of your Self-expression. They are an expression of yourself—good, bad, happy, sad, loud, soft—however, you're expressing you.

The muscles grow in strength, endurance and flexibility very rapidly. The yawn-sigh will help you ground yourself as you soar into new galaxies. Enjoy this newfound power, respect this newfound expression.

Ritual #7:
See the Nasal Edge

"See the nasal edge" is ritual number seven. "The nasal edge" is a focus point. It is the leaping off point at the end of that ski jump, the absolute perfect place for you to see sound leaving your body. Take a moment and look at Figure 6.8, so you're clear where the nasal edge is. Place the tip of your finger with your hand facing outward on your top lip, just below your nose, and hold a sound (such as HA as in "hat"), picturing that area as the focus point. Hold the sound for several seconds. Now remove your finger and put the very tip of your fingernail right on the very edge of your top lip; this will be about half an inch lower than where you placed your finger before. Now tilt your finger and your hand upward, seeing an arc. Do not tilt

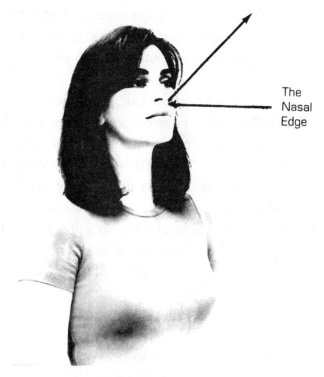

The
Nasal
Edge

Figure 6.8
See the Nasal Edge

your head, and do not tighten your neck and shoulders. Just see the arc. Create that sound again, and hold it for several seconds. See it emanating from where you are right now. Notice that it sounds different.

It might sound only a little different, but there will be a difference, and the difference is better. You may notice that it's a little richer, or perhaps it has more resonance. The tone is in some way enhanced. I call that focus on the edge of your top lip "the nasal edge." And you need to see it all the time because it will help you focus on where the voice comes from when it leaves your body. This mental image will enable you to "see" your voice and more clearly align and focus your spiritual and vocal energies. It significantly enhances your ability to project yourself with conscious confidence.

This point is the sweet spot, the spot on the tennis racket where ball and racket interconnect effortlessly as the ball hits the racket face squarely; it's that perfect swing in golf.

"The nasal edge" supports one of the major theses of Vocal Awareness, which is *focus first*. As we go through these principles of the Ritual Checklist, begin to notice that these are not merely mental exercises; they involve metaphorical principles as well. Understand that focus first is also an important metaphorical principle—not merely a vocal technique, but a life principle.

Ritual #8:
See the Arc

Ritual number eight is "See the arc" (Figure 6.9). The principle behind it is called the Bernoulli Effect. The Bernoulli Effect states that a gas or liquid in motion will exert less than normal pressure upon its surrounding environment.

Here is an easy experiment you can do that illustrates the workings of this principle. Hold a piece of paper just beneath your bottom lip and blow across the top of the paper. The paper will rise because the air pressure above it is reduced by the motion of the air. And the pressure below the paper is then sufficient to lift the paper. This is the principle of the lifting force that allows airplanes to take off and that explains all aerodynamic phenomena, from throwing a ball to ski jumping,

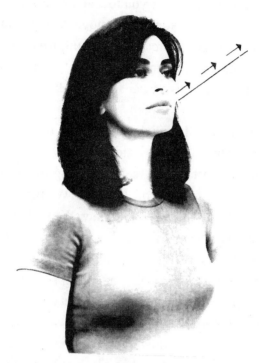

Figure 6.9
See the Arc

from playing a clarinet to singing.

While singing the vocal folds vibrate because air flow passes through them. During this vibratory cycle the vocal folds are drawn together and sound is created, and as breath (pressure flow) continues, the air passage narrows sufficiently so that the Bernoulli Effect is created. An understanding of this principle helps us to design efficient methods for training the voice.

I use an understanding of the Bernoulli Effect in two ways: first, to develop vocal exercises that enhance airflow and intensify pressure from the lungs to strengthen the vocal muscles; and second, by showing you an image of the Bernoulli

Effect, to make it possible for you to teach your mind's eye to "see" your voice. Seeing your voice move through the arc is a most powerful image that can greatly improve your voice production. When I remind my students to "see the arc," I am asking them to apply this visual image to the production of sound.

When we inhale fully and deeply, we feel the energy in the power of our breath welling up inside our body, surging upward like a geyser. But instead of freely releasing the air with the sound, what do we do most of the time? We tighten up. We tighten our chest, shoulders, tongue, jaw. We stifle our sound, our expression. By "seeing the arc," you are enabling free yet focused expression to ride the crest of the irresistible breath.

As we continue to guide the emerging sound out of our mouths in an upward 45-degree angle, we let our sound soar up and out like a phoenix rising. Eventually, it will descend on its own; gravity will bring it down, but that descent need not be part of our visual focus. When you release a ball into space, at the moment of release you are not concerned with its coming down but with its trajectory. You know it will come down. It is the same with the release of our voices.

See the arc, the soaring upward; do not worry about the distance or the volume. Just see the arc. See your vocal expression, your energy, soaring—not collapsing or descending.

I want to take you back through what we've done so far and put it all together. Sit comfortably in front of the mirror and refer to the checklist:

---

1. Thank you to my source
2. Love and let go
3. Allow a silent, loving, down-through-my-body breath and enjoy it (inhalation)
4. Release my tongue, jaw, neck and shoulders
5. Support the sound by pulling my lower abdominal muscles up and through the sound
6. The breath precedes the tone (exhalation)
7. See the nasal edge
8. See the arc

Feel those loving and conscious six- to eight-count inhalations, your hand to the jaw, your tongue released, your shoulder released, your arm relaxed as you place your hand around your jaw. See your energy moving out through the arc, leaving from the focus of the nasal edge. Enjoy this experience. Revel in it. Take your time with it. Check that three-finger extension from time to time. If your tongue pulls back, release and let it fall forward and loose once again. Have a wonderful time being you! Stop reading for a moment and just practice a bit before moving on. When you're ready, return to the book.

We will go into the last four rituals of the Vocal Awareness checklist in the next chapter. For now, please digest these eight. Synthesize them, experience them, make them a part of you. Write them out and keep them with you, referring to them as you practice—or whenever you need to be at your best. These rituals will structure your Vocal Awareness journey.

CHAPTER 7

Putting It All Together

Ritual #9:
Have a Wonderful Time
Enjoy the Work

Number nine of the rituals is "Enjoy the work." Our voice is a precious gift and opens our lives to communication, self-expression, self-esteem, and so much more. Our vocal work can be a joyous experience that brings us constant discoveries and insights. Our full-hearted participation in turn gives us continual self-satisfaction and allows for continual growth.

Voice work is meant to give pleasure. Just as poetry delights and word play is for fun, so the physical experiences of speaking and singing are a delight to the body and spirit, as satisfying to the inner physical Self as stretching to the sunning cat. By enjoying the work, we make it an integral part of our life. This permits us to make the most of our Vocal Awareness work and enriches our workouts. The challenge of learning something new becomes positive and even thrilling because we know that with our commitment, we will progress and grow. When we enjoy the work, we allow ourselves to experience the sensual and aesthetic pleasure of making sound, and we come into fuller and deeper contact with ourselves.

Ritual #10:
Take My Time

Ritual number ten is "Take my time." The importance of taking our time cannot be emphasized enough. Too often, we rush through our work. In doing so, we cheat ourselves and delay our progress. Remember—stay in the moment. The work is about process, not results.

Let yourself breathe fully and in the fullness of your time. Allow your mind the opportunity to make thorough observations. Do not hurry the work. In that 30 seconds or two minutes or 10 minutes that you manage to set aside, or the two hours that you have the luxury of working in, do not try to do it all. What is most important is not how much you do but how well you do it. Taking your time allows that adage to blossom fully.

In Vocal Awareness, we must be true to ourselves and to our own experience. Only you can determine the pace that will provide you with the optimum learning experience. You have to curb your natural impatience and a desire to see immediate results in your work. Allow yourself to take pleasure in the process; as your impatience diminishes, your development will accelerate.

"Take my time" means to take each moment at your own unhurried pace. Experience the work consciously, conscientiously and completely. By doing this, you will accomplish far more than you could ever have imagined.

Ritual #11:
Pay Attention/Deeper Listening

What do we need to put it all together? We need to begin with the eleventh principle of the Vocal Awareness checklist: "Pay attention/deeper listening." Seems like a rather simple thing to do, doesn't it? We've been paying attention to lots of things our whole lives. But have we really? The kind of attention I'm talking about involves all the elements of Vocal Awareness and allows us to put them all together. I want you to think of paying attention as *deeper listening*. Remember at the beginning of our story, I spoke of Vocal Awareness as a journey that always takes us inward, into deeper areas of discovery? Deeper

Listen deeply, inside and out.

listening therefore means that we learn to listen to the inside not merely to the outside. We listen to what our deeper Self has to say. And we respectfully learn to honor that.

So when you "pay attention" you're really experiencing how it feels to be you. Pay attention to the loving and letting go, to the breathing, to the metaphors of the checklist and not just the mechanics. *Paying attention/deeper listening is a very valuable tool for focusing and becoming the best of your Self.*

The batter climbs into the batter's box, but does the batter just swing? Of course not! He has a ritual before climbing into the batter's box and he has a ritual once in the batter's box—just as you now have one with the principles of the checklist, especially "loving and letting go." Why does the batter employ his rituals? So that he can leave one reality—that of standing in the on-deck circle, perhaps—and focus on another. So that he can pay better attention to the moment at hand—not the moment five seconds later, but the immediate moment, now.

Over the years I've worked with many professional athletes: tennis players, basketball players, swimmers, runners, football players. They all have their own rituals which, mechanically speaking, have nothing at all to do with their particular sport. The ball player crossing himself before coming up to bat, for example. Crossing himself is not going to make him a better player. The basketball player standing at the free-throw line to shoot a free-throw—maybe it's his or her ritual to dribble twice or spin the ball three times. It's not going to help the arc of the shot, but it is going to help him or her to focus, to pay better attention.

I saved paying attention for this point because it is both a summing-up and a jumping-off point. It is the place you'll most neglect. It will be the most seductive principle of the checklist because it will be the one that will go most easily unnoticed. And aside from "Loving and letting go" and "Thank you to my source," it may be the most important. Because when you pay attention, symbiotically all the other elements will come into play. If you pay attention, you're going to breathe more effectively and feel good about yourself. You're going to feel the support of the muscles and distinguish the difference between the stomach muscles pulling in and pulling up and in. Most important, you're going to be able to listen better—not just to the outside of you, but more particularly to the inside of you. That's "paying attention."

Another aspect of paying attention is to allow yourself to become self-correcting as the work continues. Vocal Awareness is an ongoing experience. It isn't black and white. It is a process. You don't wake up one day and find that you're perfect. You experience, instead, a gradual becoming.

I've been working with a very talented young woman from Japan who is bilingual, speaking both Japanese and English. She is a broadcaster for a Japanese television show produced in America and broadcast in both Japanese and English. We work on her English, of course, and also on her broadcasting skills, for broadcasting is the same in any language. She speaks English all right, but does make a few mistakes. However, no one bothers to correct her because one understands everything she is talking about. So she never gets better. And because she's so easily understood, she never bothers to correct herself. But now, she wants to become fully bilingual and speak English without mistakes, and she can—when she pays attention.

The other day, I was working with a Los Angeles automobile executive, a bright young man in his mid-30s who is on the fast track. We've only been working together a short time, so he's not quite into the routine of "paying attention." The other day, I heard him say "misconscrued." I tried to bring to his attention that he was mispronouncing the word—it's "misconstrued." Then he heard it. Before he had not been listening. When he began to listen, he was, of course, embarrassed. He was so embarrassed that he immediately began to pay better attention to his syntax, his grammar and to the way he presented himself.

I teach my students that if you make a mistake in a presentation, you have basically four options. If you don't correct it, I might think that (1) you're not very bright, and I might not trust you; (2) you think *I'm* not very bright, and you're not going to trust me; or (3) you're lazy and don't care, and I most probably won't trust you. So the only viable alternative is the fourth one: to correct yourself when you make a mistake. But the only way you're going to know when you need to correct yourself is by paying attention. Whether it is in the classroom or in the boardroom, it makes no difference. Remember, your voice is your identity.

What identity do you want us to perceive? Do you want to be seen as a careless presenter? Or do you want to be identified as a person of character and integrity?

Ritual #12:
Be My Self

The twelfth ritual is "Be my Self." Allow yourself to be in the moment and to feel the center of balance of who you are. Recognize that if the present moment is all it can be, then the result will be what it needs to be. Listen, feel, experience your passions, your desires, your fear, your habits. Experience the infinite nuances of these expressions as you begin focusing on your Self, discovering and connecting who you are, and allowing that new fulfilling fullness and self-knowledge to come through on every level.

Persona

The persona is the Self that we present to the outside world for the purposes of concealment, defense, deception or adaptation to our environment. Our persona is the outside image that we project. It was also the mask worn in Ancient Greek tragedy plays. 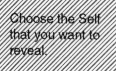 Interestingly enough, the word "person" comes from the Etruscan *phersu*, which means "through the sound." So our identity is sounded, spoken through the facial mask to project our self-constructed image to the outside world. Our vocal sound is our inner voice communicating, or striving to communicate, to the world at large. When we become adults, we think that the way we present ourselves is—well, the way we present ourselves. That's it, folks—what you see is what you get! But that's simply not true. *You have a choice. Remember, everything in life revolves around only two things*—to choose to do something or to choose not to do it. In the case of presenting who you are, you have a choice.

I'd like you to write out on a piece of paper how you think you are perceived by others. Then on another piece of paper, write how you would like to be perceived. After you have finished writing, draw what these two characters look like. They can be stick figures, representational or abstract. I've seen the most magnificent drawings, and I've seen the simplest; they're all different.

Through this exercise, you begin to tap into a deeper part of yourself. You discover things you were completely unaware of. By once again taking it from the inside and putting it on the outside, you have a chance to look at it, examine it. You are making another map, plotting a truer course for your life's journey. It's an exciting opportunity for you to discover how to make a difference through a simple and practical exercise.

As people are developing their new voice to fit this new persona, they often say to me, when listening to it in my studio without a tape recorder, "Oh, it sounds too loud," or "It sounds too nasal," or "It sounds too this or that." But then we tape it and the voice sounds just right—in fact, better than just right. Part of the confusion comes from the way we hear. Our outer ears are secondary sensors of sounds, for hearing sound on the outside rather than our sound from the inside. When our ears pick up our voices, we hear the voice after it has sent its energy out into the world, and after the sound waves have bounced off the surface in front of us and come back. The outer ear, therefore, is more properly used for hearing sound outside of us, not inside. We hear our own voice primarily through the bone conduction of our inner ear. If you really want to hear what your voice sounds like to others, cup your hands around your ears, bringing your ears slightly forward with your palms facing outward; then speak. You'll hear your voice in a very different way. This is a truer representation of your natural voice. Also, if you stand in a corner and speak directly into the corner, you will hear a clearer representation of your voice.

Choice

As you begin to examine your Self and your persona and to make the changes that Self-examination inevitably stimulates, you will find that all these negative repressive forces that are used to "being in charge" are going to rise to the surface to scare you, threaten you and confuse you—to keep you from truly emerging. Be aware: the huge "inner critic" may come up with a big sign that says, "This is phony. This is not you. *Don't believe that you can do this.*"

And you have to respond, "Don't believe that I cannot do this."

As you begin to do this work more and more deeply, you may experience vulnerable moments. When you are vulnerable, you are in jeopardy. You are closed to your true and deeper Self. Don't be. Instead, experience yourself breaking through and opening. When you're open, you're in touch with your truer and deeper Self—you're in charge. To paraphrase the author Henry Miller:

◆

Man is like an onion with a million skins. To shed the first layer is painful beyond words. The next after that, still very painful. But then, it begins to become a joy, a delight, an ecstasy. And man walks forth from the open wound he carried about with him for so long and is reborn.

That's how I want you to see yourself. Not as Icarus flying near the sun, wax melting on his wings, crashing to the earth, but as a phoenix rising from the ashes—invincible.

Consummate Communication—Personal Mastery— Wholeness

When I speak about the rituals, the breathing and the loving, it's not because I want you to have "perfect technique." The work requires technique, but that perfect technique is the by-product. The goal is to have consummate communication, personal mastery, sovereignty. To achieve this requires perfect technique. But once again, it is the result, not the goal.

I place so much importance on the mechanics of the work because I want you to pay better attention. In meditation, for example, if you're not focusing on your mantra or your breath, you're not meditating. Your mind is wandering around doing something else. So you gently but specifically are reminded to bring it back into focus—pay attention. I call this issue the "paradox of transcendence." Your transcendence to an altered state of consciousness requires consciousness; you can't be unconscious and meditate. You can't be unconscious and grow spiritually and emotionally in life. *You can't be unconscious and do this work.* The rituals of the checklist and self-correcting ingredients of the program are all designed to continue bringing you back into focus—into paying attention.

As you take this work further and deeper into yourself, you'll come farther out. You'll discover that there are fewer places to hide. But in all honesty, you're going to find that there's less need to hide because you're going to welcome the whole Self. You're going to feel the 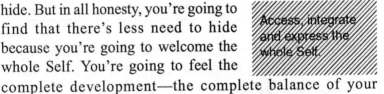 complete development—the complete balance of your androgynous Self, the wholeness, the gestalt of who you are.

One of the healthy ways a woman can express her androgyny is through speaking. Philosophically speaking, the speaking voice is the male domain, male power. Conversely, one of the ways a man can actualize his androgyny is by singing—the feminine expression of voice. This thesis comes from the Apollonian/Dionysian theories of ancient Greek literature. Many of us find that in the patriarchal and compartmental worlds we live in, we censor ourselves. A woman is supposed to sound a certain way because in learning her speech, perhaps at her mother's knee, she unconsciously began imitating certain vocal and presentational behaviors that led to her speaking as she does as an adult. And a man speaks, well, speaks "like a man." Similarly, "men don't sing." Singing shows emotion, and the learned stereotype is that we, and specifically men, are not comfortable expressing emotion. Put it all to bed. Discard those worn-out theories. All they do is keep you in your box. *Access all of you.* You don't need anyone's permission to do so.

8 percent, 37 percent, 55 percent

It's very important to listen at all times to what you're saying and how you're saying it. When we communicate with spoken language, only 8 percent of that communication is received by the listener through the words, the actual language of the communication. About 37 percent is gathered from the sound of the voice and 55 percent, the remainder, is understood from the body language. Therefore if I'm speaking on the telephone, some 92 percent of my information is communicated solely through the sound of my voice—not the content. What follows are several mechanical techniques and exercises to improve your communication and make the content of your message more effective and more easily understood.

To help you convey most effectively the 8 percent of our communication that is taken in from the language itself, let me

> Get to know your voice. Make friends with it.

first teach you a concept I call "subliminal persuasion." Read from the following prose selection. (If possible, work with a tape recorder while doing this portion of the book.) First, reading aloud, just read it as you would ordinarily.

◆

How wonderful is the human voice! It is indeed the organ of the soul. The intellect of man sits enthroned visibly, on his forehead and in his eye the heart of man is written on his countenance, but the soul reveals itself in the voice only.

Longfellow

Now read it again, employing the principles of "subliminal persuasion," which I'll explain afterward. Note the words in bold type. Please stress them in some way—louder/softer, higher/lower, etc.

◆

*How **wonderful** is the human voice! It is indeed the **organ** of the **soul**. The **intellect** of **man** sits enthroned visibly, on his forehead and in his eye **the heart of man** is **written** on his **countenance**, but the **soul reveals itself** in the **voice only**.*

The boldface helps you grasp the meaning of what you're saying. Because only 8 percent of your information will be communicated through your language, it helps the unconscious mind of the listener(s) identify the important ideas of your communication.

One also makes emphasis by pausing, by changing the pitch

of the voice, raising the pitch or lowering it, perhaps by speeding up, or by inflecting the voice down or up. Be careful, however, not to "punch" words, so that you sound like some of those hyper-expressive broadcasters. Your communication should be real and honest. Share your ideas; tell your story. Don't just "punch" a verb or adjective because it seems dramatic to do so.

The Pencil Technique

As we continue to "put it all together," I'm going to introduce you to a technique employing the pencil and separately, the two-fingers-under-the-tongue technique. We're now going to be doing yawn-sighs with words and with a pencil between the teeth. To begin, you'll read a sentence aloud, speaking it *very slowly, very nasally*—but with no tongue or jaw tension, merely effective support (seeing the "edge and arc"). You'll read with *very elongated phrases*, encouraging the sound to project over the "top of the pencil." Maintain the focus of the sound at the tip of the top teeth and the tip of the top lip. Read the sentence that follows, which begins, "When I speak, I need to be aware . . ." Notice the way the sentence is transliterated with "h's" and "ah-ee's" and the "ah's." These techniques will help keep the vowels open longer. In this way, you're going to teach the mind's eye how to sustain the voice more beautifully, as it would sustain it if you were singing. The peculiar spelling will help your mind's eye to understand, so you will then support the sound better and speak the words more completely.

Begin with two fingers under the tongue and speak nasally. Next, remove the fingers and speak over the pencil. Then take the pencil away and speak "naturally," while "visually" seeing the edge and arc and reaping the benefits of both techniques.

Are you ready to begin? Do you have the checklist in view? Is your tape recorder handy? Reference it. Ready—silent, loving breath: begin.

---◆---

WHE(N) I(AH-EE) SPE(E)K, I (AH-EE) NEED(H)D TO BE(E) A(H)WA(E)RE OF(AV) PROJE(H)CTING M(AH-EE)Y VOICE IN A VERY(EE) SPECI(H)FI(K) ARC(K). IT DOESN'T(DAZN'T) MA(H)TER WHETHER(H)R IT'S LOU(H)D OR WHETHE(H)R IT'S SOFT. THE ENERGY RE(E)MAI(H)NS CONSTA(H)NT E(E)VE(H)N THOUGH THE VO(H)LUME(H) MA(EE)Y CHA(H)NGE.

WHEN I SPEAK, I NEED TO BE AWARE OF PROJECTING MY VOICE IN A VERY SPECIFIC ARC. IT DOESN'T MATTER WHETHER IT'S LOUD OR WHETHER IT'S SOFT. THE ENERGY REMAINS CONSTANT EVEN THOUGH THE VOLUME MAY CHANGE.

How did it feel? Do you notice additional richness, resonance, focus and energy? Do you feel the benefits? Note your experiences in your journal.

As you apply Vocal Awareness in this way, *don't leave pieces out.* Support the sound, don't rush, don't tighten your neck or shoulders, and keep it "musical." Let it go high and low, but always maintain the same focus—the same edge. In other words, pay attention. It's how we put it all together.

The reasons for going high and low (as in singing) are many. Because it changes pitch, more melody is created in the speaking voice. By changing the pitch, you're also going to change the "colors" of your voice. When there are more harmonics to work with, the voice becomes more interesting.

When you feel comfortable with this exercise and can do it well, it will become one of your best tools, for immediately organizing the voice in the way you want. Ultimately, it does not even have to be done loudly at all. It can be done quite softly—in the bathroom, at the office. Before going into a meeting, just take a moment to focus and apply the technique.

At a conference several years ago in Strasbourg, France, I saw a videotape of a larynx engaged while the person was *thinking words*. You can gain great benefit *just by doing the work correctly in your mind.* You're not making sounds; thus there's no air pressure moving through the vocal folds, so they're not getting stronger. But they are becoming coordinated and, therefore, the integration of mind/body/spirit is taking place.

Now go one step further and apply these techniques to the first lines of the beautiful Robert Frost poem, "The Road Not Taken." Read the first stanza initially with no Vocal Awareness.

---------------◆---------------

Two roads diverged in a yellow wood,
And sorry I could not travel both
And be one traveler, long I stood
And looked down one as far as I could
To where it bent in the undergrowth:

Now apply the principle we've just learned. First, two fingers under the tongue on the first two lines, seeing the nasal edge, the arc, all the principles of the checklist. Tape recorder ready? Begin:

---◆---

Two roads diverged in a yellow wood,
And sorry I could not travel both

The next two lines with the pencil:

---◆---

And be one traveler, long I stood
And looked down one as far as I could

Lastly, put it back together and read *naturally* and *visually.*

---◆---

To where it bent in the undergrowth:

After you've done this, your words and sounds will feel so much nicer in your mouth. You'll feel so much fuller, so much more secure and beautiful. You and your voice will be feeling good.

In an earlier chapter, I spoke about sound being expressed emotion. I enjoy making sound unnecessarily, and I always presume I will do well. You may come to the experience with the exact opposite thought in mind—you expect it will be difficult. *Assume it won't be, and it will make all the difference in the world.* That confidence, that comfort, that security has come to me through this work because speaking and singing feel so good in my body/mind/spirit when I do them. I can't help but feel confident and have the highest Self-esteem possible because *I feel in charge.*

All these exercises can be applied as well to singing. As I've said, singing is very important to the development of the speaking voice. It adds colors, range and strength to the speaking voice. Many people have said to me, "I can't sing. I'm tone deaf." When I was teaching in the theater at the University of Southern California, I had a student in my class who *was* deaf, almost 100 percent in both ears. However, she was in my Vocal Awareness class, so she had to do the work. We began at the top of the first semester by her placing one hand on my larynx and one hand on the top of the piano. She couldn't use a tape recorder; she could only feel the vibration, so I played very loudly. She began to sing scales on pitch. By the end of the first semester, those scales became the song "Do, Re, Mi" from *The Sound of Music*, which she sang with one hand on my larynx and one hand on the piano. By the end of the second semester, she sang "The Sound of Music" all by herself. The next year she missed the first semester. She came back the second semester and sang the old pop/country hit "Blue Bayou" at a performance level. All this was done on pitch. She accomplished this simply through her extraordinary courage, tenacity and hard work.

The Three Aspects

I want to summarize this chapter by teaching you one more very important component of the work that will completely "put it all together." It is a method for learning what I call the "three aspects." The "three aspects" is a training technique that incorporates all the principles and all the paradigms of Vocal Awareness: the checklist, the exercises, etc. For purposes of explanation, we will use one hour as the block of time for practice.

The first aspect in this one-hour block will take 10 to 15 minutes. The focus will be on technique 90 percent of the time and on the beauty of your voice 10 percent of the time. Please remember that my concept of technique is the trinity, integrating mind/body/spirit (once again, not merely biomechanics). During the first aspect we warm up the voice, either doing the yawn-sighs for speaking or the vocalizing for singing. This is where the voice learns how to do what it needs to do just as an exercise. An athlete or a dancer, for example, would never just go out and compete or perform without having stretched the body. If you want to have the most effective voice possible, it stands to reason you'd want to warm it up, too. So that's what we're doing during the first aspect.

The second aspect of that same hour block of time takes 20 to 25 minutes and is about 65 percent technique and 35 percent aesthetic. This is here you will apply those H's and long vowel sounds in your spoken language and your songs as well as the principles of the pencil technique, so that you're truly impacting the musculature, the mind and the spirit all at the same time. This second aspect is a bridge, a transition that takes you from warming up to performance.

The third aspect is the remainder of that one-hour block: the performance, the presentation. The focus here is now 90 percent aesthetic and 10 percent technique. We've come full circle, and we've integrated the principles of Vocal Awareness at a professional/performance level. At this level, you must always be consciously aware, just as the tightrope walker is always consciously aware. Remember, one hour is only an example. You can do the three aspects in any length of time— even in one minute. An added note: once you have completed the first aspect, do not feel you must stay in the second aspect before going on to the third. Move back and forth between the second and third as you deem it necessary.

Always do the three aspects with all Vocal Awareness elements at hand, with all the tools in your toolbox—the checklist, the mirror, the tape recorder—so that you can listen and experience as objectively as possible to how you're doing and what you're doing, at every level, *all* the time. Do not leave pieces out. Do you see how integrated, how organized, how simple it has all become?

Some 20 years ago, as I was preparing to go to bed, a thought came to me while I was reading a magazine. I didn't want to get up and write it down, but the thought wouldn't leave. So I was forced to get up, get a pen and write it down, which I did in the magazine I was reading. The thought was this:

Voice is the only artistic experience that is both finite and infinite at the same time. It is fallible and fragile, gone in an instant, unseen, only felt—remembered from the past even a long moment ago, anticipated, sensing its future even as its present is just occurring. It's temporal, visceral, organic—such a complex, simple and beguiling transcendent state.

A few years later, I was invited to the Institute for the Advanced Studies of the Communication Processes at the University of Florida. While working there for a couple of weeks, I spoke with two of the greatest voice scientists in the world about this principle that had come through me so clearly and completely. They loved it. They believed it. During this visit, one more thought came to me: that I could substitute the words "life" or "love" for the word "voice" and achieve the same paradigmatic model.

———————————◆———————————

Life *is the only artistic experience that is both finite and infinite at the same time.* Love *is fallible and fragile, gone in an instant, unseen, only felt— remembered from the past even a long moment ago, anticipated, sensing its future even as its present is just occurring. It's temporal, visceral, organic—such a complex, simple and beguiling transcendent state.*

With this new insight, the puzzle was complete. It became clear to me what my work was really about. Vocal Awareness 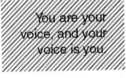 teaches about the trinity of life. Vocal Awareness is the integration of life/love/ voice—all synonyms for the same thing. The metaphor is now crystal clear. *You are your voice, and your voice is you.*

The Complete Vocal Awareness Ritual Checklist

1. Thank you to my source
2. Love and let go
3. Allow a silent, loving, down-through-my-body-breath and enjoy it (inhalation)
4. Release my tongue, jaw, neck and shoulders
5. Support the sound by pulling my lower abdominal muscles up and through the sound
6. The breath precedes the tone (exhalation)
7. See the nasal edge
8. See the arc
9. Have a wonderful time/ enjoy the Work
10. Take my time
11. Pay attention/deeper listening
12. Be my Self

As I have already said, Vocal Awareness technique is identified as a trinity—always integrating the mind/body/spirit paradigm. In observing the above checklist, you will see in this matrix the trinity principle at work. 1 through 3 are spiritually based, 4 through 8 are technically (mechanically) based, 9 through 12 are emotionally based (psychological).

CHAPTER 8

The Voice of Success: Voice in the Workplace

Years ago when I first started working with companies, one of my longtime students who worked for a major corporation said to me, "You can't go in there and tell people to 'love and let go.' You can't tell them to say, 'Thank you to my source.' That's inappropriate language." I replied, "But I cannot *not* do that. I must." And that is exactly what I have been doing all these years.

Throughout this book I have been talking about how empowering it is to feel love—to feel love for myself, for others, for the work that I do—and to express that love with a generosity of spirit that is honest and unsentimental. For me, this love is at the core of

119

everything that I do. It is the foundation of my teaching; it is evident in all the techniques. It weaves throughout this work, and it should weave throughout the workplace. This chapter deals with using your voice in the workplace—in any work, whether you are a lawyer, a mother raising children, the president of a large company, a classroom teacher, a broadcaster. Whatever your work, you need to use your voice.

When I bring Vocal Awareness into the workplace, people often say I have opened up a window for the fresh air to blow in. Vocal Awareness is such a departure from the generally myopic vision of how the workplace should function. A student of mine was visiting an engineering office in Colorado. He noticed that everyone was talking behind everyone's back and that the man who was the supervisor was so invested in being the boss that he wouldn't communicate with any of the employees. My student talked to this supervisor and mentioned many Vocal Awareness concepts. He said the supervisor's whole face just lit up when he was told, "Your company could be much more successful if you all started talking to *each other* and with each other rather than *at* each other." It had never occurred to this supervisor that there was another way of running the office.

In my corporate seminars, I create an intense, loving and demanding environment that works as a learning environment. During these Vocal Awareness seminars, you can feel the energy in the room shift. It becomes quieter, more peaceful. People find a positive way of being territorial and are open rather than defensive. They feel safer. Yet so many places of business do not allow people to feel safe; the employees are shut down and creativity is shut out. The seminars restore that sense of Self and safety. The safe seminar-learning environment becomes a microcosm of what the traditional workplace can be.

And why shouldn't the workplace be a safe environment? Most of us spend more time in the workplace than in any place else, except in our beds asleep, and sometimes we even work more hours than we sleep. If where we are spending so much time is not a joyful place, or at the very least, creative and comfortable, then we need to do something about it.

In our work—as in our life—we exhibit patterns of territoriality. To put it in the vernacular, we sort of "pee around our tree." Staking out our turf, setting up our lines of defense and never venturing beyond. We do not offer love or allow it in or think about it very often. Work and love! It seems almost an oxymoron—as though the workplace is an inappropriate place in which to express love or to enjoy respect.

You should only work in places where you are respected and where you can relate from your power, your sovereignty. I work with the largest executive search firm in the world. Vocal Awareness is very important to these out-of-work men and women because people are facing a most challenging time in their lives; they feel perhaps their weakest, their most disenfranchised and most disempowered. They need to know some degree of sovereignty so that they can go and apply for a job with a sense of confidence. Instead of walking in with anxiety and fear of rejection, they can enter with their chest high, hold a hand firmly, look the interviewer clearly in the eye, and come from their power. The evaluation comments these individuals give regarding Vocal Awareness are extraordinary. What these sessions do for these individuals is to provide them with a sense of Self and self-empowerment.

Take Ownership—You Are
Your Best Investment

Our society is a hierarchical one, our culture largely patriarchal. There is so much abuse—not just men abusing women, but parents abusing children, straights abusing gays, race set against race, the stronger brandishing their power over those beneath them. So in the workplace we unconsciously hold our breath when going into a meeting, or we feel we have to say "Yes, sir" and "No, sir" all the time, or we feel forced to put up with a compromising situation.

The perception is that you have no choice. Which is another way of saying we have to settle for the way it is. But we don't have to settle. We do have a choice. Remember every single thing in life revolves around those two things, to choose to do something or choose not to. You can choose, like a racehorse with blinders on, to run as you are told, down the path, unaware, not using your peripheral vision, not "seeing from your heart," tuning out and turning off. Or you can make choices. You can talk to somebody about a behavior that offends you, or you can recognize that this is a behavior belonging to that individual and does not need to be taken on by you. You can change the situation by leaving, or you can change the situation by rising above it and perhaps inspiring others. But you never, ever have to settle for an ugly situation and you never, ever have to close your eyes to it because when you do, you shut down, you abandon your Self, and you forsake your power.

I have learned through Vocal Awareness that in our society, *two of the greatest personal fears are the fear of owning our power and the fear of being abandoned.* Dealing with these fears is a two-fold challenge: first we must become aware of our rights; and second, we must become conscious of owning our power so that we do not 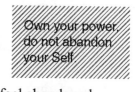 abandon ourselves or allow ourselves to feel abandoned.

You must invest in yourself. You do so by owning your power. When you attempt to deal from a position of weakness, you attract those who fit into your weaknesses—like a key into a lock—and you attract those who prey on weakness. You attract a boss who intimidates you or one who uses you. When you come from your power, you do not create such self-sabotaging situations. You recognize that you are worthy and deserving; you do not have to fight, and you do not have to protect your territory. You can merely *be*.

A tenet of Vocal Awareness is that we do not need to settle for that which compromises us, but we do need to be able to recognize it, accept it, move through it and beyond it.

Albert Camus, the existential philosopher, relates the Greek myth of Sisyphus and how, when Sisyphus realized that he was to roll the rock up the hill for eternity, it no longer bothered him. He conquered his fate, as it were. A young actress and client of mine came in and told me, "The other day I was so upset. I came from my power and I asserted myself with my personal manager. I felt it scared my manager and I possibly had lost him. I became terrified that by being in my power I might actually lose him. But later I discovered that it clarified things between us." Unless you meet people in your power, you will lose them anyway. Otherwise, you are attracting the key-in-the-lock weaknesses of others. Ultimately, the only worthwhile way to deal with people is from your power—your sense of Self and what is right and just for you.

Being You in the Interview

One of the most important times for you to remain empowered and to "be" rather than "present" is in the job 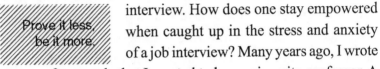 interview. How does one stay empowered when caught up in the stress and anxiety of a job interview? Many years ago, I wrote as one of my goals that I wanted to be a university professor. A few months after setting down this particular goal, I received a call from the Theatre School at the University of Southern California, asking if I would like to come in for a job interview. They were looking for a voice teacher. When I had written down my goals, I had written specifically that I did not want to be an assistant or an associate professor, but that I only wanted the position of professor. During the interview, I made it clear that I would only be interested in the position of professor and that I did not want to be an assistant or an associate. And so I became an Adjunct Professor of Voice in the Theatre School of USC.

You may wonder that I should have been so assertive in an interview, but if you are coming from the ownership of who you are and if it is clear to you that you are deserving (on a realistic basis), and if you are clear about what you want, in all fairness to yourself you must state it. I teach those who study with me that we are all in the education business. We have something that is needed. The world does not know that, so we have to educate the world—or the future employer—about what it is we have to offer. To do this, you have to stay in your power, stay true to your goals, and communicate honestly and straightforwardly.

On a similar note, around that same period of time I was back East, where I visited a friend who was at the world-famous drama school of Yale University. As a favor, my friend took me into the administrative office of the Yale Rep to see if anyone had time to meet with me (I was only on the East Coast briefly). The associate dean made time for me. During the first few minutes of the interview, however, I quickly saw that this man was meeting with me merely as a favor; he was taciturn, not forthcoming, and not making it easy for me. Because I was in my power and was using my "deeper listening," I saw from his body language that he was annoyed. I also saw that I was not hitting his "hot" button, but I kept "listening" and looking for it. Ten or fifteen minutes into the interview, I hit it. Finally he said to me, "The next time you are coming to this area, let us know. I will have you conduct a master class here at Yale." I did. He did. And he was so pleased with the first class that he said, "We would love to have you any time you are in the area. By the way, our Yale rep voice teacher said she would like to study with you." This dean became a lovely friend and supporter, even writing me a letter of recommendation that I use in my press kit. It has been a joy for me to recall that because I was able to stay empowered, I was able to reach this gentleman, make vital business connections, and even find a good friendship.

In addition to learning to stay in your power, it's important to take the very practical steps of preparing and rehearsing for the interview. I have been helping a young man who is a senior economics major at UCLA, a thoughtful, hard-working, caring individual. He came to work on his language and presentational skills, for he had never felt confident in public situations nor did he feel he was communicating with a sense of maturity. Now that he is about to enter the full-time job market, he has to learn how to interview. So this fine young man has been role-playing with me. He records phone conversations and tapes practice interviews at home, listening to his grammar and syntax and observing himself closely. He is trying consciously to be the best of himself within the construct of these professional interviews and to see himself in the role of businessman, not the role of student. He is working actively to shift into a newly emerging identity. Working with this conscious awareness, rehearsing and practicing as he is, he will be successful in his job interviews.

Yes, the prospect of an interview is daunting, but if we can look at it as an opportunity to share what we have to give and as a challenge to demonstrate the newly developed sense of ourselves, the interview can be a positive experience. We never know but what the next interview may bring us is a good friend.

Our Mandate: Self-Esteem

I have often considered the greatest problem in our society to be a lack of self-esteem. If we felt good about who we were, we would not need to harm others, or to take from others what does not belong to us. We would not be compelled to conquer the weak or destroy another. That may seem a sophomoric and naive statement, but that is the reality. Accept the truth that *if we felt genuine love for ourselves, we would be able to feel love for another.* In our security, we could function more effectively and communicate more clearly.

For some time, I have been working with a gentleman who has been a mid-level executive at the national headquarters of a major car company. He is a devout and spiritual individual— a sweet man, a big man, soft-spoken, about 6'3" and 230 pounds. He had been a football player in college. I recognized immediately that he needed to be able to command his self-esteem and to communicate from the basis of the physical image that he projected—solid, secure and larger than life—rather than in the way he presented himself—insecure and vulnerable. I sensed that those above him in his company saw him as weak and ineffectual and that he might eventually be pushed out of the company. After all, he mumbled, and he avoided eye contact when talking with you. His voice was small. He had a tight jaw and an inexpressive face. A big burly man, he had gained some weight in recent months, and his suit was just a little tight.

My relationship with his company stopped for a few months until the new fiscal year. My client was in touch with me during those months because we had developed a good personal relationship, and I was helping him in some other areas. One day he called to say that he was being forced out of the company, even though he was one of the major creative forces behind the extraordinary success of this company. He explained that a new division president had come in. The new president was shifting him to another department in a move that was clearly a demotion and the first step toward forcing him out. And this was happening all because this gentleman did not esteem his power, did not esteem himself, nor did he project the image that he was capable of projecting.

In an earlier chapter, I said that perception is reality. If we perceive something to be true, it is, whether it is or not. I had been trying to change my client's perception of himself so that those around him would perceive him as powerful, but we were too late. It will be a loss for the company, but that company's loss will be another company's gain. In the interim, my client has become stronger and more secure and is beginning to present himself on the basis of his Vocal Awareness persona statement.

In my seminars I do a fun thing. I say to the group, "Give me your perceptions of what you think of me, good, bad or indifferent, and be as candid as you want." They tell me. Then I change. I talk to them in a very different way, in a gruff, intense way. Next I talk to them in a rather supercilious way, in a whiny little voice; I put my hands in front of my fly, looking completely insecure, and then I ask how they perceive me.

But no matter what is their perception of me, I know who I am. My self-esteem is intact, and I know how I choose to present myself. You can make choices about how you wish to be perceived. You can value and esteem yourself and give yourself permission to be your Self.

Who Are We—Really?

The Ritual Checklist gives Vocal Awareness its structure, and this structure supports you in your daily use of your voice—in your daily expression of your Self and your identity. My clients become totally involved in the rituals. A receptionist I work with at a major corporation has the checklist on her computer screen. She also keeps a second copy by her telephone to remind her and reinforce the Vocal Awareness persona principles. If you were to meet this young woman in the lobby, you'd see a lovely smile, a wonderful warm and secure person.

But interestingly enough, if you were to meet her somewhere else, you would be introduced to a fragile, insecure, uncomfortable person. She and I have spoken many times about this, and she has discovered why she feels so comfortable in the lobby, behind "her" desk, at "her" computer screen, with "her" bank of telephones: it's "her" turf. She owns the space. She has been on that job for many years. She rules over her territory and does it beautifully. But when she leaves that space, she leaves her strength and security behind.

During one of our sessions, she told me of an experience she had had while traveling with her sister in Mexico. The pickup truck in which they were riding went out of control and off a cliff, rolling over many times. When the truck finally came to rest at the bottom of a ravine, she was able to pull herself out of the truck. But she discovered that her sister was trapped under the truck. What did my client do next? She lifted the truck off her sister and saved her sister's life! Since she told me this story, it has become our metaphor. It has become the symbol for the woman that she is—a woman with the strength and courage to succeed with nobility and power. This is the woman she can be at all times. "Why do you have to become a groundhog when you leave your desk? Why go back into your hole because you've seen your shadow?" I tell her, "You are strength incarnate. Why do you allow yourself to make any other choices?"

In the workplace, this woman chooses to stay empowered and integrates Vocal Awareness into every aspect of her activity. As a result, she is successful in her job. She does not have to be reminded that when we speak on the telephone, 92 percent of our communication is gathered from the *sound* of the voice. So many of us are unaware of the impression we are making as we speak on the telephone, even though we spend a great deal of time on it. Picture yourself with the receiver next to your ear and the mouthpiece two or three inches from your mouth. You are sitting slumped over the desk, your neck and shoulder tension running amuck, no support from the lower abdominals. You are holding your breath, not paying attention to vocal mechanics, and trying to do "business as usual." How can we possibly have good Vocal Awareness under such circumstances? Yet that is how we spend so much of our time in the workplace—both on and off the phone.

The other day I was calling a friend at a local hotel, and I could not understand the operator. I called back because I was not at all sure I had the right number. The operator spoke so quickly and carelessly that I simply could not understand what was being said. When I work with the employees of a hotel such as the Ritz-Carlton, for example, I work first with the executive committee, the leadership of the hotel, and with PBX, the people who answer the telephones. They are the first line of contact anyone has with that property or, in fact, with any place of business. The employees who answer the telephones represent the company, sight unseen, to the caller. If the phone is answered in an indifferent, robot-like manner, the caller may see the business as one that is indifferent and uncaring.

The Breath and Positive Change

We have so many opportunities to apply the Vocal Awareness principles in the workplace. How do we get to the point of always making the most empowered choice? We achieve that by requiring ourselves to do the Vocal Awareness work in this very precise and structured way every day.

We go into the workplace and we pull out our checklist. Before we go into the meeting, we look at the checklist. I tell my broadcasters that the most important part of any broadcast are the three seconds preceding it. They may have warmed up, but if they do not use their Vocal Awareness techniques in those three seconds when the floor manager or the producer is saying into the earpiece, "We're coming to you in three, two, one"—if in that moment they are not loving and letting go and conscious of their silent and loving breath, then when the red light goes on, they are going to be and appear unconscious. This three-second preparation applies to all of us in all work situations. Any time we need to be focused and at our best—before walking into an important meeting, before making a critical phone call— this three-second ritual will empower us and bring us to conscious awareness. Imagine if you embraced the importance of owning the sound of your voice and the discipline to enhance it, what kind of impact you could have on others.

That's all very well, you say. But I have to pay my bills. My job takes all my thinking time. I cannot risk losing this $4.50-an-hour job. I cannot risk offending someone. What am I supposed to do?

Recently, I had a conversation with a woman who works in the prop department of a motion picture studio. Most of the prop department employees are in the Teamsters Union, and she feels isolated and trapped and is finding it hard to be strong because the men are harassing her constantly. I told her of another woman who had dealt with a similar situation, a woman I had met in one of my week-long seminars. My seminar attendee was probably in her early 50s and had originally been a seventh- and eighth-grade science teacher. She had left an abusive marriage and moved to Chicago, where she found a job on an assembly line as a machinist and became a union organizer. She was the only woman in the shop, yet she became the shop steward. Immediately, she was confronted with the reality of sexism, and because she expressed support for ethnic groups, she also faced all kinds of racial prejudices.

While on that job, she went through another abusive marriage, and it was not until a year ago, after many years of being in this ugly situation, that she finally found the courage to move out of the stress-filled job, out of the abusive marriage, and to the Northwest, where she has been for the last year. At the end of the Vocal Awareness seminar she wrote a three-page fairy tale about a little girl and a dragon. As the fairy tale came to a close, she realized that she now knew, totally and completely, that as long as she stayed in her loving breath, she would be able to stay in her conscious awareness and quench the fury of these fire-breathing dragons. It was an extraordinary awakening, and as she told the story of a little girl, seemingly alone and frightened, lost in the forest of her story, becoming a mature woman, a queen, commanding and in her power, her voice reflected the metamorphosis—moving from high-pitched childishness to full-voiced empowerment—something she did not recognize until it was pointed out to her.

The point of this story is to encourage you to recognize, first of all, that change is possible, but secondly, and most important here, that there is a connection between your life in the workplace and your life in your home. If you are going to close your eyes to an abusive situation in the workplace, you will deny it as well in your home. If you are going to close your eyes to something that is going on 8 hours or 10 hours a day in the workplace, you are going to close your eyes at home as well.

If you see your job is upsetting you or that your partner is abusing you, you can also see that you cannot and should not stay in such a situation. Your personal life and your working life complement each other. As the workplace becomes more loving, more empowering, so will the home place.

So many people cannot see a way to move on, or even a way to begin to move. Fearful of risk, they ask nothing for themselves. They cannot say, "I have to leave one night a week early so I can go to class." They are so trapped that change and movement seem impossible. But movement starts with breath, breath begets communication, and breathing and communication together move you into positive change.

Vocal Awareness recognizes that if we are to have what we want, if we are going to have life on our terms, we have to take responsibility for the terms and face the risks. If I choose to be unhappy, then I am choosing to be unhappy. If I choose to stay on a job where I am miserable, then that is my choice. Once again this may sound simplistic, but as Harry Truman said, "The buck stops here." After all, it has to stop somewhere. The more completely you take responsibility for your choices, the more you come from your power, the more Vocal Awareness becomes a part of the way you are, the more often you can know success in the workplace.

> You don't get to choose how you're going to die, or when. You can only decide how you are going to live, now.
> —Joan Baez

What is success? It's giving love and receiving love and being yourself, being true to yourself, being who you want to be, not settling for where you are but accepting it and moving beyond it to a new dimension. Remember, the Vocal Awareness journey is about always going inward. There, every day can be a success. But success is also about attention to detail. It is, in fact, predicated on an unremitting attention to all the details that we have spoken of—the down-through-the-body breath, the visualization, the loving and letting go, the surrender, the focus.

Success is further determined by attending to its substructure, the three T's: timing, talent and tenacity, the most important of which is tenacity. Timing is achieved as we listen more deeply; our talent is enhanced as we attend to details, and all comes to fruition through tenacity—as we stay with the work through all of the challenges and assaults that life offers us.

People are so cut off from their dreams and their hopes. It is so seductive to be present for someone else's acceptance of us, rather than being who we are. But you have a responsibility to your Self, to be always the best that you can be and to take that professionalism into whatever job and whatever work situation you move into. If you go into the workplace with these Vocal Awareness principles, you can make ripples. Ripples can become waves, and waves bring change and movement. You can affect both yourself and your workplace in a positive manner, and in this way you can find success in the workplace.

CHAPTER 9

Seminars: Like a Rocket to the Moon

R ecently I returned from a seminar I have been conducting annually at an internationally known retreat facility. I'm always so moved when I return from these seminars. In the brief period of one week, an extraordinary metamorphosis takes place.

My students arrive on a Sunday afternoon, and we begin the work that evening. All sessions are two hours in length. Monday and Tuesday we have three two-hour sessions, with time out for breakfast, lunch and dinner. Wednesday includes two two-hour sessions, with the evening off. Thursday is another three-session day. We finish on Friday morning, and by noon the retreat is over.

The seminar is entitled "Vocal Awareness—Empowerment Through Voice." I have had students come from all over the world—from the United States, from Russia, Germany, Southeast Asia, Switzerland, Canada—you name it. What a wonderful experience for me as a teacher to spend an entire week with a large number of such dedicated people. In my private practice, I generally spend an hour or so once a week with one person. This week with a large group is an intensive one, where meaningful work is accomplished.

Beginnings are always so interesting for me—whether those in a week-long course or in the three-hour seminars I conduct throughout the United States and in Canada and Europe. Many different people come together with their own set of expectations, and each is unique. Whether 15 people or hundreds attend, there are many agendas; yet nobody knows what Vocal Awareness really is. The group sees me as something akin to a bullfighter—am I going to get gored or will I survive? Some think of me as a bit like Icarus. How close to the sun will I fly before the wax melts on my wings? I love the challenge.

Our Sunday night work begins with an overview; the breathing process, an explanation of what Vocal Awareness is about, of what empowerment through your voice really means, and what they are going to gain from the seminar. I also ask what these individuals want for themselves. I ask them to begin to think about the week's program, the creation of a personal statement, the drawings. And thus the work begins. Monday morning we come back together. In the first two or three sessions, we spend a great deal of time on breathing—integrating the "breath consciousness." We work individually and in groups. We begin liberating neck and shoulder tension and tongue and

jaw tension, and systematically laying out the 12-point Ritual
Checklist. This Ritual Checklist is, of course, always the
foundation of Vocal Awareness. It provides the structure upon
which the entire relationship with Vocal Awareness and its
relationship with you is based.

In addition to yawn-sighs, traditional vocalizing, singing
and the Ritual Checklist, sound meditation is introduced to
deepen contact with the Self. To borrow from the catalogue
that advertises the course, the goal of the work is to develop
creatively. For this to happen, the following must occur:

◆

*Creative energy is accessed, feeling is enhanced,
the capacity to feel is increased, sensory sensitivity is
heightened, a channel for expression is determined and
content for creative expression is identified. In many
traditions, the throat is the center of creative power.
The voice represents this power and thus has the
capacity to help access our full creative expression.*

So for the first two days, we develop the breathing and the
yawn-sighs. By the evening of the second day we begin working
with the spoken word, and the pencil technique is introduced.

Awakening and Metamorphosis

The individuals I work with in my seminars, many of whom
are on a path of Self-enlightenment, represent to me a
microcosm of society. They come from all walks of life. They

are dentists, therapists, stockbrokers, physicians, nurses, lay people, teachers. Though they all have individual agendas, all, in varying degrees, face the same "vocal" challenges—tongue and jaw tension, neck and shoulder tension, shallow breathing, TMJ, all the usual array of fears. Each is a "normal" person.

Initially, my responsibility is to awaken them, to make them aware of all the "baggage" they carry with them. Generally they are aware of some of it, but at a superficial level. They must also be made aware of the reality: that they can get rid of this baggage. Within a few short days, they can "unpack their bags" and leave them in the closet forever because they won't ever need that stuff again on this journey. Doesn't that seem astonishing? It used to also seem impossible to me, but over the years I have found it is true.

When I first began doing this retreat, I recognized that if I created the kind of cataclysmic change I desired in such a short period of time, I had to have a dramatic catalyst. That catalyst turned out to be the very environment where I was working at the time. This exquisite compound where these annual seminars are held is set on a cliff overlooking the Pacific Ocean. It includes many acres of grounds with beautiful vegetable and flower gardens, steps to the ocean, a meditation room, a stream, a waterfall, woods—you name it, it has it all. I have the group participate in this environment in a very special way.

On Wednesday, I guide my class on an unusual journey (remember, Vocal Awareness is always a journey—inward, never outward). We spend half a day in silence—no words at all are spoken—listening to the power of nature's voice. I lead my group from point to point, spending 20 minutes to half an hour in different parts of the grounds. We listen, feel, tune in and tune out, and an amazing transformation takes place as the group starts hearing and listening differently. Several hours later, we go back indoors and play recordings of great music with great singers. Not all the singers I choose have profound voices. Some, frankly, have simple voices, but that is also part of their journey. While experiencing the music, participants draw and write their impression of the day's events, including the music they are then listening to. People are deeply moved. The emotion is intense—there are tears, silent hugs.

The next morning they share their observations, drawings and writings. Everyone is drawn closer together. The afternoon session introduces singing, and by this time, the bond is even greater. The commitment of each to oneself and to the group is solid.

Friday we have our closing session, a sort of graduation, as it were. Everyone is asked to prepare something—a mission statement that may have been written that week, a persona statement—anything that speaks of the contribution the week has made and what it is he or she wants to take away. People draw, dance, write poems, compose mission statements and more.

In one of my seminars, an individual who came from England to take my course was greatly challenged when attempting to sing in tune with the group. I stopped the group work to work individually with him for about 10 minutes, and I helped him to sing five or six notes on pitch, albeit with a great deal of difficulty—but he was able to do it. Yet what he did 18 hours later, on Friday morning, was one of the most astonishing things I have ever observed in all my years of teaching. After he had read us a poem he had written, he sang

"Amazing Grace" full out, with his mouth wide open, his tongue released, his consciousness, his sovereignty fully engaged. As they say, there was not a dry eye in the house.

One man presented artwork he had made from stones, twigs and earth from the woods. He then turned his back to the group and sang the first verse of "The Rose," his voice sounding very muffled. People wondered why this was, until he turned around and showed us that he had stuffed a washcloth into his mouth, representing how he had come in on Sunday, feeling that he was suffocating and unable to speak or communicate in full voice who he was or what he wanted. Facing the group, he then pulled his tongue with the washcloth and sang the second verse of "The Rose." For the third verse, he embraced his complete consciousness and sang with joy and abandon.

This gentleman's mouth on Sunday had been so tight that I could have done "chin-ups" on his jaw. Now it seemed as though it had opened all the way to his belly button. Astonishing! People were sobbing—genuinely moved because the experience had been so extraordinary. As they watched and participated, the week's events accelerated to a stunning crescendo. Everyone had chosen to commit. Everyone took wonderful risks because each knew, first, that I was there for them as a teacher, protecting them and guiding them lovingly and effectively. But secondly and most importantly, *they recognized their commitment to themselves and what it took to achieve the level of work and success* that I promised they were capable of accomplishing. Every single person made that full and total commitment. Every single person invested fully and drank fully from the well. All left deeply moved. One woman said that she had had one of the most profound experiences of her life. Another man said that he recognized that his life had been changed. So you see why I call this chapter "Like a Rocket to the Moon"!

What Are We Talking About?

In another seminar, the one given for the Los Angeles education-based company, the three-hour course is entitled simply, "How to Improve the Sound of Your Voice." I'm told that a class like this normally attracts 20 to 30 people; I've been drawing a minimum of 55 on a Monday night and as many as 92 on a Saturday morning. Recently, in New York City, I attracted a crowd of 101 on a Wednesday night. The workshop is obviously tapping into an unrecognized desire in the community to which we all aspire: to master the sound of our voices. But the seminar is so much more powerful than that, and in the three hours we spend together, the group is taken through experiences that lead them to a recognition of what we are really talking about. We are not talking about voice (that's the metaphor). We are talking about the Self—about empowerment.

The advertisement for the class states:

◆

Participants will learn how to develop a natural and dynamic voice, to breathe correctly; to create a "presence" in their speech, to enhance their image, to look and sound better, to build Self-esteem and Self-confidence and to develop their singing voice. [They will] improve communication skills [and learn how to] create a lasting impact.

The ad closes with, "Come learn how to make your voice a winner." But I always know that what people are really showing up for is to learn how to make themselves winners, or better yet, how to recognize that they already are.

In these seminars I bring to their attention an interesting paradox that I have observed. It is a paradox that recognizes that the way most of us behave—appearing shy, introverted, fragile, uptight, fearful, etc.—is designed by us (we think) to protect ourselves. "I am too afraid to come out further. I am too afraid to let you know who I am. You might harm me or I might be harmed." The interesting paradox is that by behaving this way, we jeopardize the very essence we are trying to protect, and we expose the Self that does not want to be seen as fearful, tense, uptight or fragile. *If you do not want to be in jeopardy or appear to be in jeopardy*, you have to behave in a totally different way. *You have to behave in an empowered way.* But to do this you have to risk, and that is the rub. It is the difference between opening the door and taking the journey. We think we are afraid to open the door, but what we are really afraid to do is explore the Self and take the journey.

A Personal Story

In some of my seminars, I risk telling my participants a very personal story about my life. It begins with a discussion of my family and the fact that I never knew my father. The only information I had of him came from a picture I had seen in my home. He was dressed in a World War II army uniform. My mother told me he had passed away after being injured in the war.

Shortly after I got married, my wife suggested that I call the Veterans Administration to see if we could get more information about my father—perhaps find some money that was due my mother. I called the V. A., and they told me they had an active file on him, but that it didn't mean anything—merely that nobody had ever called on the claim.

At that time my sister-in-law worked for a branch of the Federal government where she could easily access this information. I gave her my father's name and where I thought he had been born or had lived prior to the war. She came back with an address and a phone number. I immediately went to my mother and asked her why I had been misinformed. She then explained to me that I had been born of a wartime romance; after I was conceived and just prior to my birth, my father informed my mother that he was not in love with her and that he had a hometown fiancee who he planned to marry after his discharge. But to "legitimize" my birth, he married my mother a month before I was born. My father was discharged, the divorce obtained, and that was that. He asked my mother to tell me nothing of him, and she never did. My whole family knew this story but I did not.

On learning all this, I embarked upon an extraordinarily empowering journey. It began with a Sunday morning phone call to my father. When he picked up the phone, my first words were, "Hello, Mr. Joseph. I believe you're my father and I'm your son." As you can well imagine, dead silence ensued for quite a few moments.

Finally he spoke, and we proceeded to talk for about an hour. I learned some important health information and that I had four half-siblings, none of whom knew of me. The woman he had returned to marry did know about me. She had passed on 10 or 12 years after their marriage, and now he was remarried. His current wife also knew about me. He expressed a desire to know about me and my family and so I wrote letters, sent pictures, and called a couple more times—but he never replied. The last time I called, his wife said, "He doesn't want to know that you exist. Drop it!" I said politely, "I'm sorry, ma'am, but I'm never going to drop it. Someday I will show up on your doorstep," and I gently hung up.

About ten years ago, I was on my way from Atlanta, Georgia, to Akron, Ohio. Coincidentally, a client of mine had done my numerology for me on the way to the airport that morning. I do not know anything about numerology, but she wanted to do it. Not knowing what I was about to do, my client said that this day was going to be a day of completions and beginnings, and it was not going to be an easy one. What a soothsayer she was! Before reaching Akron, I stopped in the city in which my father lived. At 9:00 P.M., I landed on his doorstep. Earlier I had decided that I did not want this to be merely an intellectual experience; I wanted it to hit me between the eyes as viscerally as possible. And boy, did it! As I stood on his front porch, in spite of the illogic of what I was doing, I looked at my left breast pocket. This experience was so intense, I thought it was going to be like a Warner Brothers cartoon and my heart could be seen pounding through my shirt.

I knocked on the door.

The door opened, and before my right foot was even in the living room, the terror was over. My heart stopped pounding. I could breathe again. It was an extraordinarily important metaphor that helped change my life. I discovered that we think we are afraid to "open the door," but that is not the issue at all. *When we open the door, we will be able to deal with whatever is on the other side. What we are actually afraid to do is to take the journey, to begin.*

I spent 15 minutes with my father, took a couple photographs, and left. He asked me not to tell his children about myself. I chose to honor that, and until two years ago at this writing, that was the end of the story. I never contacted him again.

Then two years ago, my wife and I were addressing holiday cards with our family picture on them. Out of the blue my wife asked, "Should we send one to your father?" I thought about it a moment and said, "All right." I wrote a note on the inside, addressed the envelope and stuck it in the mail.

A couple weeks later, I was picking up our youngest son from school on the last day before winter break. He was late getting out of class, and because we have car phones, I was able to let my wife know that I would be late arriving home. My wife answered the phone as she was pulling into our driveway. She told me there was an older woman stalled out in front of our house. Over the phone I heard the woman say, "Hello, Rebecca," and my wife say, "Pardon me, do I know you?" the woman said, "I'm Helen, Helen Joseph."

This woman was my father's wife. She was wintering about eight miles west of our home. She had received our holiday card and had it in her purse. She happened to be driving south on the street immediately adjacent to our corner. When she saw our street, she turned, pulled in front of our house and, I swear to you, there her car died. Rebecca immediately put Helen on the car phone, and Helen proceeded to say, "Your father died six months after you left." One of the paradoxes of my life has been that I never knew I had a living father and I never knew I had a dead one. Remember those two enormous issues I spoke of earlier, ownership of our power and fear of abandonment? There they were, hitting me square in the face, once again. I realized that I had to take my power for myself, and I had to confront this abandonment once again. So I said to this lovely woman, "It's time to tell the children about me." She gave me the phone numbers, and a couple days later, I spoke with my half-siblings for the first time in my life. That holiday I had nieces and nephews call and wish me a happy holiday and call me "Uncle Arthur." The following summer we had a family reunion, and I met my family for the first time. My whole life and my family's life changed as well—all because I was able to take a risk, all because I wanted to have life on my terms.

I share this story with people in my seminars not just to grandstand, but to speak personally about what it means to be there for oneself and the significance of the risks sometimes taken. I share this story also to illustrate that it does not cost as much as you think. In fact, it costs less. In fact, there is nothing to lose. There is no cost, just extraordinary gain and unbelievable empowerment. My story often proves to be just the element needed to bring people to the level where they are inspired to work even harder on their own discoveries and their own journeys. I hope it does the same for you.

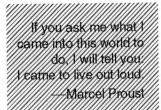

If you ask me what I came into this world to do, I will tell you: I came to live out loud.
—Marcel Proust

CHAPTER 10

Vocal Hygiene:
Creative Solutions to
Vocal Problems

The length of time necessary to master the Vocal Awareness techniques will depend on what the student brings to the practice, the extent of the dedication and how deep-seated the poor habits. Some problems such as dry throat, dry mouth, hoarseness, sore throat, too much saliva and that notorious malady, TMJ (jaw tension and teeth grinding) can be handled more expeditiously. Even stuttering and lisping can begin to be dealt with, using some of the simple, straightforward measures that deal with what we might call "vocal hygiene." What do you do when you have a cold, when you travel, or when you are tired? All can affect your voice, as does your emotional state; but you can take simple measures to protect your voice under these circumstances.

Warming Up

Our larynx, or voice box, is the smallest muscle in the body. If you were a professional athlete or a professional dancer, you would always stretch your body before competing or performing. And every day, when you go out in the workplace using your voice to represent who you are, you must think of yourself as a professional voice user. It is not unreasonable, therefore, to ask you to think about warming up your voice before you set forth. The warm-up does not have to be a big deal; a few minutes can suffice. But when you do not feel well, a warm-up is more difficult. When you have a cold or sore throat or are hoarse, use your voice as little as possible. Put yourself on at least 12 to 24 hours of complete vocal rest if possible, locking yourself away in the proverbial closet. (This is the only time, by the way, that I will tell you to put yourself in the closet.) If that is not realistic, do not think that you are saving your voice by whispering; you are actually working it harder. Whispering is performed by a part of the muscle called the crycothyroid. It is a tiny part of the muscle that comes from the lower, rear part of the larynx (Figure 10.1). It is not the strongest part of the vocal mechanism and therefore it wears out a lot faster. So although you may think you are saving your voice by whispering, you are really making matters worse and exhausting the vocal muscle even more.

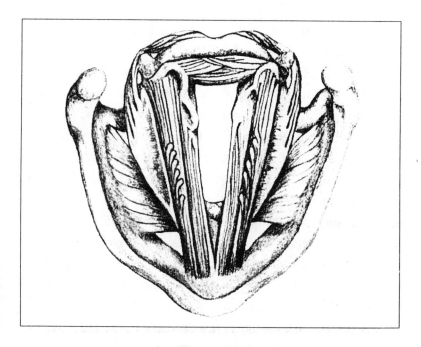

Figure 10.1
The Larynx and The Vocal Folds

Stay Conscious

When you do not feel well vocally and/or physically, the most important thing to do is to take more time to breathe. Try to allow those six-to-eight-count silent inhalations more and more consciously, and more and more lovingly. Slow down your speech so that you have more time to engage the conscious mind to coordinate, to be there for you. It will be, if you train it to do so. What do you want to be able to do with your conscious mind? You want to be able to see, specifically, the edge and the arc of the voice. Support the voice, specifically; try not to rush your speech; try not to speak too loudly, but keep the voice at a comfortable dynamic level, all the time lifting that arc just a little bit higher.

Notice the extreme diagonal of the image in Figure 6.9, page 93; it shows you that you want the arc to be even more extreme than usual. You might practice this with a tape recorder and listen to yourself speak in different ways to get into good speaking habits, feeling the edge and that extreme arc. Locate that "internal lift" and the feeling that the soft palate is lifted way, way up inside, seemingly as far up as your eyebrows. Some people refer to it as an inner smile within your mouth because you are always "lifting" inside the interior of your mouth. It will take some consciousness in the beginning to do this, but after a while it will begin to happen all by itself and to sustain itself. It is quite remarkable. Note that as you do this, the abdominal muscles are working better, too, for you are supporting your Self, physically and emotionally.

Take Your Time

When you do not feel well and you need to warm up the voice, you want to do it modestly—not too loudly, not too fast, not too high or too low—just modestly. Gently place two fingers under the tongue, or pull the tongue gently, or do the pencil exercise gently: very nasally, very slowly and only for a couple minutes, without any dramatics. Be very specific and quite slow, making sure that as you do the vocal work you are integrating the mind/body/spirit connection. Make sure that you are really slowing down and not tensing.

This gentle approach is necessary because when you do not feel well, the body compensates. You tend to speak more frugally, with worse posture; you tend to let the head dip, the shoulders tighten, the breath shorten, thinking that you are protecting yourself. All of this happens unconsciously. Instead you need, once again, to train yourself to speak much as a classical dancer walks—always lifting, always aware, always keeping the mind/body/spirit connection so that everything works as effectively as possible.

The Throat

One of the worst things you can do to your voice box is to clear your throat. Clearing the throat badly irritates the vocal mechanism, wearing it down, and is much like grinding gears in a car. To function efficiently, the vocal folds need air. Clearing your throat cuts off the air and hurts the voice. When you feel the need to clear your throat, you need instead to build up saliva in the mouth, which sometimes occurs when you get nervous, then you may want to cough gently, with a rather breathy cough, putting air through the cough and not coughing percussively or with a hacking sound. The gentle approach will probably clear the mucous of the vocal folds and give you the relief you are seeking.

Sucking on lozenges can also be helpful. Grether's Black Currant or Red Currant Pastilles, an over-the-counter brand of lozenges made in Switzerland from an old English recipe, is available in some drugstores and markets. They contain glycerin, and the glycerin is extremely soothing to the vocal folds. The old-fashioned Smith Bros. Cherry Lozenges are also fine. Stay away from menthol-coated drops, as they can sometimes irritate the vocal folds.

Years ago one of my students, a wonderful singer-dancer-actress, was performing at Rainbow and Stars at the top of Rockefeller Center in New York. She thought she was doing a good thing for herself by taking bee pollen. Unfortunately, she developed an allergic reaction to the bee pollen, and both her vocal tract (her pharynx) and her larynx became so inflamed that I could not even vocalize her prior to her show. It was a very scary experience for her. This extraordinary performer had been with me 13 or 14 years, however, and she had the Vocal Awareness technique down to a science. I told her exactly what to do, and she did it. If you were to have heard her speak without Vocal Awareness techniques, you would never have thought it was possible for her to sing. When she went out to do her first of two sets, I told her, "You really have to see the edge and the arc and be aware of your breathing—not only when you sing, but when you speak. Keep the neck and shoulders all released, the support there," and I reminded her of all the points of the checklist.

Because she had studied and practiced so diligently over so many years, she was able to strongly and masterfully integrate her mind/body/spirit connection. She went on stage and gave one of the finest performances of her career. She did not enjoy her performance as much then as she usually did because she had to concentrate so hard, but she did not "miss a trick." She did not cut any number; she did not change any of the high notes; she did not do anything less than give the best of herself possible. And the Vocal Awareness technique and her ability to own it made her performance possible.

But the point of this story is to be really careful about self-doctoring. My student thought that by taking bee pollen she was doing something to help herself, without knowing that she was creating more problems.

More Tips

If you travel a great deal and have to use your voice energetically in business as soon as you arrive at your destination, try to speak as little as possible or not at all while on the airplane. When I was in graduate school, we conducted an experiment in a voice science class that included taking a sound-level meter into the cabin of a jet. According to the meter, the stress on the vocal folds when speaking in the plane with the engines churning was equivalent to shouting when standing by the afterburner of a jet. Speaking over the noise level in the airplane places a great strain on the larynx. Notice the next time you fly how many hoarse flight attendants you run into. If you must speak while on the plane, speak as quietly and with as much edge and arc as possible.

Women need to be aware that the vocal folds are affected by their menstrual cycle. If edema (swelling) is a problem during menses, edema will occur in the vocal folds as well as in the rest of the body. Furthermore, a woman is most susceptible to vocal abuse during her period. It is especially important for women who must use their voices during menses, whether singing, acting, speaking or even making an informal presentation, to take more time to warm up the voice and to warm up much more thoughtfully than usual. The voice is not as flexible as it normally would be. Of course, some women are severely affected at this time, others minimally, some women not at all; the response to that particular time of the month is individual.

All of us, men and women, need to drink plenty of fluids; at least eight to 12 glasses of water per day, at room temperature—not too cold and not too hot. Drinking honey and lemon or warm tea is nice and feels good, but anything too hot or too cold affects the mucous membranes around the vocal folds adversely. Placing a hot compress on a wound, for example, causes the blood vessels around that area to expand. Conversely, placing a cold compress on a wound, for example, constricts the blood vessels. The same thing happens to the blood vessels around the vocal folds. The vocal area needs to be kept as neutral as possible. Drinking anything too hot or too cold affects the vocal folds and surrounding area, and does not allow the area to stay neutral.

Some Causes of Mucous

As harmful as the temperature extremes of liquids is the drinking of sodas. Regular sodas, such as Coca-Cola, contain one teaspoon of sugar for every ounce of soda. A 12-ounce can of Coke, then, means drinking 12 teaspoons of sugar. This high sugar content creates much mucous in the vocal folds.

Alcoholic beverages can sometimes have the same effect. Beverages such as red wine contain tannin, used in the processing of the wine, and can cause increased mucous. (White wine does not have this effect.) If you need your voice to be at its best, it is wise not to drink red wine immediately before a performance or presentation. Grain alcohol, vodka and beer can cause a histaminic reaction and create mucous as well. Coffee can dry out the mucous membranes and also cause problems.

Dairy products are notorious for producing mucous. Consuming milk and cream (though not cottage cheese) can contribute to mucous.

More Serious Problems

If you are told by an ear, nose and throat specialist, or otolaryngologist, that you have a vocal problem, such as nodules or granulomas, for example, always get at least two, if not three, opinions before acting. Several years ago I had a client who had been a famous athlete. He had a habit, after a performance, of drinking quite heavily and occasionally smoking some marijuana. For some time I had been telling him not to do this, especially when he was performing, because it could affect his voice adversely and even cause him to lose it. One night has was performing and singing in his nightclub act. He had two shows: during the first set he sang relatively well, though he noticed a little hoarseness. Then almost instantly, between sets, he lost his voice, and he could not go out for the second show. Of course, he was in a panic. So we tracked down a laryngologist, "out in the middle of nowhere," and he went by himself to the doctor. He came back later that night and told me that the doctor had said that he had nodules. I assured him, "You no more have nodules than I can jump off buildings and fly; you are having a histaminic reaction to all the vodka you keep drinking. I have asked you not to drink." Of course, he replied, "But the doctor saw them." I said, "The doctor is crazy. If you have nodules, I swear to you that I will write you a check for all the money you have spent with me over the years." I was dead serious. And I could make this kind of wager because I knew intuitively that this doctor was wrong.

In any event, at 1:00 A.M. I called and woke up a world-famous New York otolaryngologist, Wilbur Gould (who has since passed on). Dr. Gould told me to bring my client in the next morning, which I did. Thirty seconds after the start of his examination, Dr. Gould told my client, "You do not have nodules; you are having a histaminic reaction to all the vodka you keep pouring down your throat. Quit drinking." Needless to say, our athlete/performer was relieved.

The larynx is the most complex muscle in the body, the smallest muscle in the body (compare the size of the larynx with the length of the hamstring, the long muscle at the rear of your thigh and the longest muscle in the body). The larynx is the only muscle in the body that works only with air. It is a very complex thing to analyze and to observe. My client was put on vocal rest for a couple days, told to take a particular prescription to shrink some of the swelling and, of course, advised to quit drinking. He did—at least long enough to repair his voice, for within three days he was back on stage.

TMJ

TMJ conventionally refers to the habit of grinding the teeth and the excessive tension carried in that area. TMJ stands for temporal mandibular joint, that joint just by your ear. When you open your mouth wide, you can feel the space being created by the temporal mandibular joint. As mentioned before, with 56 moving parts, it is the most complex joint in the body. The jaw, some voice scientists say, is capable of anywhere between

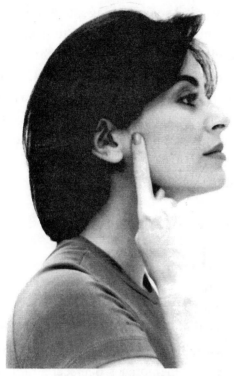

Figure 10.2
Removing Tension in Your Jaw

6,000 and 10,000 pounds of force per square inch. The area is equally the carrier of tremendous stress and tremendous tension.

It is vital to good vocal production to release tension in the temporal mandibular joint area, and you can begin to do so by gently massaging the area of that joint with your fingers as often as possible (Figure 10.2). Massage for three or four minutes, particularly at night before you go to sleep and in the morning upon awakening. Try as well some deep pressure massage— not to the point of causing pain, but just to create relief, going around in a circular pattern and then reversing the pattern, along with pulling downward. As you massage, tell yourself not to clench your teeth at night. Make an attempt to sleep with your mouth gently closed, so as not to dry out your throat.

Do all of this regularly before going to sleep. If possible, go to sleep to soft music, classical music or relaxation tapes. Do this consistently for a couple weeks, and your TMJ problems will cease. The severest case that I have seen took one month to cure. The TMJ may flare up again in a moment of stress, but now you have a technique to get rid of it.

Smoking

Smoking is obviously a very bad habit on many levels, but it is even more destructive to the professional voice user. It is not so much the smoke (unless you are smoking marijuana) as it is the heat. Subjecting the vocal folds to 2,000- to 3,000-degree heat dries out the mucous membranes severely. To protect themselves, the mucous membranes oversecrete mucous. As the mucous increases, tissue layers are formed on the vocal folds, thickening the muscles, reddening and enlarging them as tissue layers are built up, one upon the other. As this happens, the throat has to be cleared more often. This in turn irritates the vocal tract and the vocal folds even more.

Nodules and Granulomas

Nodules are often referred to as nodes. They are a common condition that occur in the posterior third—the upper third—of the larynx, which produces the higher part of your voice. Nodes can develop in 24 hours or over long periods of time. Nodes are the result of stress or, more often, of using the voice improperly, with bad vocal technique or not support, by speaking too loudly or too fast or with too much tension, and so forth.

Granulomas are more commonly referred to as contact ulcers. They occur in the anterior third—in the area that produces the low voice. They often result when the larynx, in trying to create a low voice, or extensive coughing or shouting pushes the speaking voice too low for its natural pitch range. The larynx is forced against the hyoid bone (Figure 3.2, page 33). Over time an ulcer, or a hole, forms in the vocal folds, severely limiting vocalization. These conditions must be treated by an ear, nose and throat specialist, or otolaryngologist, working in conjunction with a speech pathologist, speech therapist or a superior voice teacher. If caught early enough and treated carefully with vocal therapy and good retraining of vocal technique, they can be healed. If these conditions are not dealt with properly, surgery may become necessary.

Fatigue

When the body is fatigued, the voice is generally the first outward sign of this fatigue. Vocal exhaustion is heard immediately, expressed in breathiness, hoarseness, a lack of support and energy. This is a time when you are most susceptible to vocal injury and therefore must be acutely aware of good technique—specifically, of good Vocal Awareness technique. Better support, better breathing, better Vocal Awareness all around are required.

Lisping and Stuttering

Stuttering, of course, is a psycho-physical challenge, it usually has an emotional as well as a physiological cause. The great American actor James Earl Jones has always been painfully shy as well as a lifetime stutterer. Responding to a query about his stuttering, in an interview in the Los Angeles Times (December 19, 1995: F8), Jones replied:

◆

My voice is a gift that often doesn't work. I still have difficulty getting thoughts out, so my goal is to say something with clarity. I left the church at the age of 14 because I couldn't do Sunday school recitations without the kids laughing . . . But the great Olympic runner Wilma Rudolph had serious leg problems. [Dancer] Gwen Verdon had rickets as a child. Demosthenes put pebbles in his mouth and became a great orator. If you acknowledge a weak muscle and exercise it, it can define your life.

Aware of his weakness, Jones consciously conquered it. Stuttering can be managed and even eradicated through conscious awareness, by integrating mind/body/spirit, and through good Vocal Awareness technique. I have helped many through the years.

Singing is a wonderful way to counteract stuttering problems. Singing helps those who lisp as well as stutter because singing intensifies pressure flow. At the same time, singing strengthens the muscles, creates better coordination and better timed coordination; the voice is engaged in the elongated vowel sounds of singing rather than the spasmodic use that occurs in speaking. When singing, the vocal folds stay stretched longer because pressure is being held longer to hold out notes. Singing also feels good. It raises the endorphin level, and makes the individual feel healthier and happier.

Yawn-sigh exercises help both those who lisp as well as those who stutter. Another exercise requires making a long Zzzzz sound, making the tip of the tongue vibrate with intensifying pressure as it produces the Zzzzz sound more specifically. The same exercise can be done with a Vvvvv sound, or with any of the voiced consonants. A voiced consonant (V, D, B, Z) is a sound that vibrates in the vocal tract—for example, V versus F, D versus T, B versus P, Z versus S. The unvoiced consonant is a sound that does not have the same vibratory intensity. This intensified pressure flow requires good abdominal support. Tongue and lip tension are therefore released, and the entire vocal mechanism functions more easily and efficiently.

I hope that this chapter has been helpful in terms of giving you good, hard (albeit limited) data about the voice and vocal hygiene, about certain vocal pathologies and vocal therapies. With self-attention and self-awareness and through the wisdom of Vocal Awareness we can put ourselves on the road to good vocal health and maintain it for the rest of our lives.

CHAPTER 11

The Healing Voice: The Magical Power of Sound

This chapter is about connecting with yourself on a deeper level. You have heard me say numerous times throughout this book that voice is power, literally and figuratively. It is vibration; it is energy. I want you to use this energy for yourself in ways that may be new to you. It is important that none of this seem intimidating to you or too scary. Let these concepts embrace you. Allow yourself to ignore your inner critic. *Just experience the experience.* Trust me a bit longer and trust yourself, too, as you discover parts of yourself that you did not even know needed to be healed and as you discover new ways

Be at peace and at one with yourself.

of being at one with yourself. In this way you will hear more distinctively your inner voice.

Norman Cousins describes in his book *Anatomy of an Illness* how he healed himself with laughter. Laughter, for me, is to singing as crawling is to running; for me, working with the voice and speaking and singing are the beginning of a profound process for developing my well-being. But here I am not dealing merely with the production of sound, but with sustaining sound at a deep emotional, spiritual and physical level. As you move yourself more and more deeply into yourself and hear more distinctly your inner voice, you will understand this and you will come into a new at-oneness with yourself. You will do all this as you focus on your breath, your sound, your experience in the moment of that experience, remembering always that your sound, your life, is sustained with your breath.

Lawrence Kushner, the contemporary Jewish thinker, gives the letters of the name of God as "Yod," "Hay," "Vav" and "Hay" in Hebrew. He says they are frequently mispronounced as the word "Yaway." But in truth, the word in unutterable, for this word is the sound of breathing. The holiest name in the world, the name of the Creator, is the sound of one's own breathing. This is consistent with the Old Testament translation that refers to the appearance of God as "the soft, barely audible sound of almost breathing." (See Chapter 5.) When in the 20th century we explore ancient Buddhist philosophies, we find these are talking about the same thing, speaking about the sanctity of the breath in the consciousness of the moment.

This is the critical point: if one is truly to have sovereignty, if one is truly to live a life of joy and passion, a life on one's own terms to the best of one's ability, *there must be sovereignty.*

You must understand how to stay with and within yourself, and you do this by staying with the breath and within your breathing.

A student once asked me, "Why do you use the word 'sovereignty'? Why don't you use the word 'ownership'?" But if we are to live life on our own terms, we must be sovereign. Merely to "own" one's life trivializes and mis-states the significance and value of the work involved. You must recognize the nobility of your life. You need to recognize and respect and revere what it takes to live a life, even a simple life. What you may call an ordinary life requires extraordinary commitment. To be the best of yourself requires commitment, dedication, vision, focus-release.

Dan Millman is well known for writing the book *Way of the Peaceful Warrior*, a title that alludes to the discipline that is necessary to live even the "ordinary" life. In his latest book, *The Laws of Spirit*, he lists 12 laws, just as I list 12 rituals. They include the law of balance, the law of choices, the laws of process, presence, compassion, faith. These laws help the reader to take step-by-step approaches to the daily living of life. As such, so the 12 rituals of Vocal Awareness are created to give a structure and a guiding discipline that you might better respect yourself and reflect upon the moment and be the best of yourself—not present yourself, but simply be the best of yourself.

Nothing you want to achieve in life happens without work. None of it happens without commitment, dedication, vision and focus, and none of it will happen at the level that is possible until you dedicate time on a regular basis to stillness within yourself. That time can be devoted daily or semi-weekly, but it needs to be devoted regularly to the process of going inward.

I wish I could say to you that you could do this while you are washing the dishes or driving the carpool or working at the office. Ultimately you will be able to do so, and that is the whole point of the work. Initially, however, as with anything else, it takes practice. Do not be waylaid by, "I can't make the time. I'm so busy." Turn it around and tell yourself, "I cannot *not* do this. I cannot afford not to make the time." You will find, as has been mentioned before, that it is not the journey that frightens you, but the fear of change and of beginning the journey. Opening the door is the first step in that journey. Stay with this chapter, and you could find a significant key to the unfolding of the rest of your life.

Let's begin. Sit or lie quietly and begin silent and loving breaths. Feel them move deeply down through your body, slow and rich. Feel as though you are inhaling the fragrance of a wonderful rose. Inhale more and more deeply. With each inhalation, you inhale the beauty and the richness of the rose.

Recognize that powerful forces are at work as you meditate. You do not have to know what they are. You do not have to believe from an empirical basis. Just do the work and suspend that left-brain, hyperactive, inner critic. Suspend all judgements. *Suspend all need "to know" and just do it.* Feel and listen to the awakening that is taking place—not what will take place but is taking place. It is unfolding every moment of the day, every moment of your life.

There is a lovely book entitled *Zen in the Art of Archery*. It was written in 1953 by a German philosopher, Eugen Herrigel, who taught at a university in Japan between the two world wars.

While in Japan, he mentioned to a friend that he would like to study archery, and his friend introduced him to a Zen master. The entire first year of Herrigel's archery training was spent on learning to breathe. Not even learning to hit the bull's-eye. Three or four years later into his study, Herrigel could barely hit the target, let alone hit the bull's-eye. Impatient with what he felt was a complete lack of progress, Herrigel complained to his master and was told by him:

Do not forget that even in nature there are correspondences that cannot be understood and which are yet so real that we have grown accustomed to them, just as if they could not be any different. I will give you an example which I have puzzled over. The spider dances her web without knowing that flies will be caught in it. The fly dancing nonchalantly on a sunbeam is caught in the net without knowing what lies in store. But through both of them it dances, and inside and outside are united in this dance. So, too, the archer hits the target without having aimed.

Herrigel goes on in his book to recount the exchange that ensued between student and master, and finally says, "Then you ought to be able to hit it blindfolded." So the narrative goes on and the master takes him to the shooting arena that evening and asks the student to turn off the lights in the target stand, and merely illuminates the target with a single candle flame. We're told it was so dark, that one could barely see the outline of the target, let alone see the bull's eye. The master proceeded to shoot two arrows.

The author continues, "When I switched on the light in the target stand, I discovered to my amazement that the first arrow was lodged full in the middle of the block, while the second arrow had splintered the butt of the first and plowed through the shaft before imbedding itself beside it."

The master then said, "The first shot was no great feat you will think because after all these years I'm so familiar with my target stand that I must know even in pitch darkness where the target is. That may be, and I won't try to pretend otherwise. But the second arrow which hit the first, what do you make of that?" Everything matters—nothing is insignificant, merely subtle. In subtlety lies the opportunity for profound change and growth.

Now you might ask what possible relevance does this anecdote have to you—what does this possibly have to do with Vocal Awareness and with your own sense of Self or empowerment? I assure you, it has everything to do with it. Consider the significance of what the master is saying to the student: that he can consistently do this, shot after shot. This story is not about the results. It is not about the payoff or the product. It is about the journey, about being in the moment and focusing on the moment.

Everything matters—nothing is insignificant, merely subtle. In subtlety lies the opportunity for profound change and growth.

You will learn to recognize that you are in the "dance," that you are exactly where you need to be. So you will learn how to be in the moment. By staying in your breath, in the moment, within the consciousness of your edge, arc, support—your *Vocal Awareness*—by staying within the consciousness of your empowerment, you will come to trust that you are exactly where you are supposed to be and will be able to consistently and effectively focus your attentions in that moment.

The foundation, the support, the structure, the security you now have will open you to a previously untouched knowledge. You will open to a previously unattainable recognition to find that you can "eat your cake and have it too." You may not find this tomorrow at five or next Thursday at seven. You may not be able to hit the target today, next week, next month, next year, but that is not the point. If you adhere to the inward journeying and to what I am saying and continue to follow this very simple step-by-step process on your inward way, be assured that the results will take care of themselves. Just as the archer hits the target without having aimed, you can always be the best of yourself and succeed at all that you choose to do.

If you read any further, you must feel centered. Find your centered place. Begin from that centered place to do some gentle closed-mouth hums—your pitch does not matter. Do not rush. See the nasal edge. See the arc. Feel your support.

Notice if things suddenly become more complicated as you are being asked to make sound. Is it like the archer trying to hit the bull's-eye before he can even pull the bow string back? Do not be ahead of the process. Take one step at a time.

Do not be afraid that you are being asked to juggle too many balls at one time, and do not assume that you do not have the ability to do so—you do. If the balls fall down, you can simply pick them up and try again. This is my way of saying that you may notice your breath becoming a little shorter. You may find your tongue and jaw, neck and shoulders becoming a little tense. Loosen the jaw, let go of the tension, and keep on with your sound.

Begin to *visualize that sound moving out through the arc of your voice*. It moves right out through the arc and soars into the universe. Enjoy it. Feel the energy moving and soaring. While the energy is moving out and up, *feel the emotion releasing down*, guiding images through your body as you *release all of the tension* down through your toes, out through your fingertips. Visualize what the energy looks and feels like. Give it shape and form. Put the book down once again and just do this for two or three minutes.

Once again, your return to the book signals that you are ready to move on, so let's add another piece. This time I want you to add an image, a beautiful white light coming from the area where your third eye would be. Send your sound right through the light of the third-eye spot along with your breathing. While doing so, continue to release all tension, maintaining the breath, slow and loving, in six- to eight-count rhythms. Enjoy! You might even begin to open the sound up to a HAW. If you do so, allow the tongue and jaw to release forward, lying gently against your bottom teeth—no tension at all. Do this for two or three minutes, and do not worry about doing it perfectly. This is not about perfect. Just enjoy the experience of the moment.

As we continue further on our journey, you will notice that you are going deeper and deeper within yourself, and that even as you do so, you are learning to maintain a degree of objectivity. You can hold onto more information at the same time; you can keep more energies in balance. You *can* juggle more balls at the same time. Now that you feel more confident and—I hope—more comfortable, we can add another image.

Now I want you to see another beautiful white light coming from your heart, soaring out into the universe to meet up with the stream of light coming from the third eye, and hold them both in focus. See the converging light as a bridge. Allow yourself to be comfortable. You might change the vowel sound to a HEE. Or you may choose to keep it as a HAW or even HAH. Do not, however, create product. Do not seek results. Just be in the moment, feel the moment. Once again, practice this for two to three minutes.

Now I want you to hold these images in place as you continue to read. Feel the breathing. Continue to see the arc of light soaring out from the third eye and the light energy moving from the heart center to meet it, while hearing my words inside of you, my energy and my hand guiding and supporting you. Do not be scared. It's all right.

I am now going to add another image. I want you to see a serpent entwined around your head. I do not know how big that serpent is for you. (If you experience any fear, you may later want to write your fears on a piece of paper so that you can more clearly identify them.) When I first saw my serpent, it was not small; it was rather significant in size. Feel that serpent encased around your temples. When you see it, recognize it. Feel it, then ask it to uncoil itself. Watch it uncoil and crawl out on the beam of light from your third eye. When it is fully engaged and resting out on that beam of light, continue reading.

I now want you to see another image—a blue light that comes from your throat, coursing up and down your body. Your throat center, or your throat chakra, is called also the will center. See this blue light as your sword of might. Take it in your dominant hand and with your sword, sever the beams of light from your third eye and from your heart. Follow those beams of light with the serpent attached as they are released out into the universe, never to be seen again. Do not be frightened.

When you can no longer see the serpent, repeat the following statement:

◆

Lord God of my being, I have released this snake back into the universe, for it has served me well, giving me great teaching on limitation. But I have learned the lesson and I surrender it now back in to the God force.

When you feel comfortable with what you have just experienced and when you can feel yourself once again—regulating your breathing if necessary, feeling the loving and letting go, sensing your thank-you to your source—close your eyes, go inside, and rest quietly for a moment.

As you rest, feel the beautiful white light that came from your heart continue to warm you from deep within. Also feel warmth and healing light from within your solar plexus, deep within your stomach wall. As you become comfortable with that light, I want you to feel it shooting out through your navel, embracing and surrounding you as in a chrysalis, in the womb-like enclosure. Feel as though you are floating in amniotic fluid, safe and secure. You are really floating within your own energy, within your own source. As you feel this energy swirling around you and the release of all bodily, spiritual and emotional tension and conflict, let the energy move back down inside you once again and feel it coursing throughout your body.

Recognize that this energy always has been within you and always will be. It is your energy.

When you are sure of the power of this truth, focus once again on the light within your solar plexus and say out loud, with conviction, "I am one with the light." Feel these words resonate within you. Then send these words to an even deeper source within you, with an even deeper and more loving breath, and repeat once again, "I am one with the light."

Lastly, with all your knowing at your disposal, with all the strength of who you are, with your reality balanced in the consciousness of your awareness, affirm with total acceptance: "I am the light."

This is a simple but profound visualization/healing meditation. You can repeat it as many times as you need to, if that serpent comes back again, for example. Each time you meditate this way, you will see the serpent become smaller, until finally, you will no longer feel the need to do it again.

As you begin to do this work, you may notice anxiety. You may notice discomfort. You may get dizzy or experience fear. It is okay. Do not let any of these stop you. If you feel yourself panic and that you do not have the strength to keep going, stop. Come back to it at another time. But if you feel you have the courage to keep working at that moment, notice if your pulse is racing or your breath is becoming more spasmodic, shorter or faster. Control it with your breath. *You will always mitigate all fear, all anxiety, by mastering your breath.*

If necessary, force yourself, gently but commandingly, to get back into your slow, deep, loving, six- to eight-count, down-through-your-body breath. Require of yourself that it happen. Where there is fear, there is doubt; where there is doubt, there is not God consciousness. You will always be able to find your way back out of the fear by returning to your breath, but you must do that consciously and deliberately.

If real trauma emerges for you, share it with someone you trust. Write it down, reflect on it, and let go of it. Deal with it; do not ignore it. Each time you go into this place, you will experience more and more enlightenment, more and more ability, and you will feel safer. Believe me, this is true. You can metamorphose terror, fear and anxiety into joy by feeling love in your breath. You can turn the blackness into light.

If you want to recite the previous meditation into a tape recorder and then play it back while meditating, you may find this a good way of staying conscious and integrating the work more thoughtfully, more consistently, more effectively.

Years ago, on New Year's Eve, I led a sound meditation in Mexico City with a group of individuals at the top of the Pyramid of the Sun. We followed it with another on New Year's Day. While we were holding hands in a circle with our eyes closed, I was awakened to a block in the circle of our hands, in the energy of our field, a few feet to my left. I opened my eyes and observed an individual trembling severely. This young man was in a state of great fear. Yet I sensed that he was enjoying the most wonderful bliss. The thought that he would have to come back from his journey into the bliss and lose the bliss was overwhelming him with terror. Without breaking the chain, the energy aura, the litany of sound, I went over and worked with him and helped him to release his fear. This was an epiphany for him. He was able to understand that through loving and letting go and a down-through-the-body breath, he could journey into and out of the bliss whenever he wanted to.

Do not be afraid to take this journey. This is a process, this journey, that we take step by step. Many meditation techniques employ breathing. Many techniques employ sound. Once again, remember that in Vocal Awareness we are conscious of the emotion that bases our breath and sound as we integrate the mind/body/spirit trinity.

Leave this part of the work for a moment and visualize yourself in your daily activities. See if you can hold onto the serenity that you are now feeling. Just as I asked that young man in the circle to hold onto it and return to the now, so I am asking you. See if you can remain serene while visualizing yourself at your desk at work or making dinner for your family, teaching in a classroom or heading a sales meeting, or doing any of the tasks of your daily life. See if you can read this narrative, visualize the images, and stay in this moment all at the same time. Notice that you can, and that it is easy.

Take your journey step by conscious step

Earlier in this chapter I said that it takes work to live even an ordinary life. But look how quickly you can begin to organize the mind, to engage in more than one activity at the same time, to be in the past, present and future all in the same moment because they are always peacefully co-existing anyway. We do not always know that, so we feel scared and threatened. But keep remembering to stay in the power of your breath, in the power of the moment, and notice that perhaps as you read this, you took a loving breath. Through this breath your body is telling you it welcomes and recognizes the truth of what you are reading. Whenever you panic, go into your deep and loving breath.

How do we take and create a moment of meditation, a moment of spiritual oneness in the workplace? Is it even possible? Even practical? The answer to both these questions is that of course it is. Set a routine for yourself. When you get into the parking structure at work, for example, before leaving the car, sit for 45 seconds to a minute and do a "Cliffs Notes" version, as it were, of this work. Have your checklist visible. Feel the silent, loving, down-through-your-body breath. Do a moment of gentle, closed-mouth humming yawn-sighs, seeing the edge and the arc and feeling the tummy pulling up and in, not from the perspective of making sound, but from the perspective of feeling expression. See that wonderful light soaring out from the third eye. Feel emotion release down through your body, releasing all tension. As you close, say thank you to your source, get out of the car, and go to work.

Do this meditation also in your mind. This is a variation that can be done while sitting at your desk just before you have to make a presentation, before you walk into the classroom—anywhere at all. Do this variation for 45 seconds to a minute, but do it all in your mind. Remember that the vocal folds are stretching in response to your thoughts, even when you do not make a sound. Make the sound only in your mind, and you will find significant benefit.

You can take your "portable" meditation with you anywhere just by doing it in this simplest but very empowering way. This can work even if you are in an "unconscious" moment, or in shock. Your boss has just screamed at you; people have been rude to you. Or when you are thrown off center or someone is deliberately throwing you off and threatening you. You regain your equilibrium through your conscious awareness, through your deeper listening, and it is all based on the silent and loving breath, that breath of God described in the Old Testament.

The work of Vocal Awareness, whether in singing or public speaking, is built on theme and variation. We take a small piece and build on it. For example, the meditation you just learned had at least four variations: one in the car, one at the desk, one with sound and one without.

It is important also for you to know that through this work, you will soon have the confidence to become your own teacher. That is imperative. I am here merely to open the door and to show you how to do the work yourself.

Experiment with this work, but always do it in a safe place. After you work in this way, always ground yourself. Settle back "into" your body and consciously reconnect to your environment. Have some food to eat; have some nice music to put on. Do not jump right into a frantic pace or get in the car and drive off. Give yourself a few minutes.

When you come out of these meditations, do not come out of them too quickly. Your awareness will be so heightened that your energy field may feel the way your legs do when you get up after having sat on them and they "fell asleep"—all pins and needles. Your experience will be so heightened that you may look like one of the characters in a "John Keane" painting. (Remember that San Francisco painter from the 1960s who painted all those people with big eyes?) You are going to feel as though you are walking around with saucer eyes, seeing and sensing so much. It can be very startling at first. But you will come to welcome it.

Do not be afraid of surrendering to who you are. Do not be afraid of being the best of yourself. As we close this chapter, make a promise to yourself (or if you cannot make the promise yet, consider when you might be able to make it). Promise yourself that for one week you will begin every day with a gentle five-minute meditation of loving breath and gentle sound, visualizing the third-eye image flashing out through the arc and the heart image soaring out through the arc, and while the energy is soaring and the emotion releasing, you are listening and feeling. Stay within that. Commit to doing it for five minutes at the top of every morning, perhaps before you get out of bed, or perhaps in the shower. Commit to doing it within the first hour of your day. Commit to doing it, and watch what happens. You can always be the best of yourself and succeed at all that you choose.

Commit to repeating that process in the microcosmic form of one minute either with the sound in the car in the parking lot or with no sound at work. Do this twice a day for one week. Merely *one* minute each time—a total of 14 minutes. Watch what happens! When you come out of these moments, always

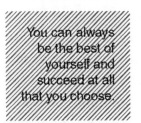

close them with a thank-you to your source and a thank-you to yourself. Feel the breath that emerges after that, set the intention for the day of living within your power, and live within the consciousness of the gift of who you are.

Revere yourself. You show yourself that you do so when you honor yourself; you show yourself that you honor yourself when you make this commitment. *Be at peace.*

CHAPTER 12

Why Sing?

◆

All my being is song. I sing as I draw my breath.
(An Eskimo saying)

O ne of my favorite songs is the Disney classic, "With a Smile and a Song," from the first Disney-animated feature, "Snow White and the Seven Dwarfs" (1937). The music is by Frank Churchill, the words are by Larry Morey. It sings:

◆

With a smile and a song,
life is just like a bright sunny day,
your cares fade away, and your heart is young.

Everything is in tune
and it's spring and life flows along,
with a smile and a song.

This deceptively simple and seemingly benign thought in part answers the question posed at the beginning of this chapter.

I have lectured and taught throughout the United States and around the world and I have never met a single individual—not one person, young or old, man or woman—who, when engaged in a conversation about it, hasn't said to me, "I'd love to sing."

Why do we all love to sing? For one reason: singing gives us pleasure. It is the most hedonistic art form there is. We sing because it feels good. Whether we recognize it or not, singing brings us physical, emotional and spiritual pleasure.

You have heard me say that sound is expressed emotion. Singing is both about exclaiming joy, and tapping in to release deeply held pain and trauma. When we sing, we are expressing our deepest emotions, those for which mere words are inadequate. The sound of singing comes from the deepest core of our being. Even when we sing of our sorrow, at another level we are expressing our joy and awareness that we are alive and able to feel.

When we sing, we give of ourselves most fully, for we are communicating our deepest feelings. We reach within ourselves to touch our emotion, are in touch with ourselves, and so communicate our emotion and our Self.

In my travels, the classes I have taught have ranged from private lessons to seminars with over one thousand people in attendance. The participants come from all walks of life—lay people to professional performers. Folk, pop, theatrical singers to classically-trained concert artists. From toddlers as young as one-and-a-half to individuals in their nineties. All of these people have many things in common. They may all come from different walks of life, have different personal goals in mind, but the common threads that weave throughout my work and bind them to Vocal Awareness is the pursuit of their truth—their "reason for being."

Singing is the single most important factor that makes the Vocal Awareness work so successful. Individuals may fear their voice, may say they "can't sing," but let me reveal a secret to you: Every single person on the planet wants to sing and can sing. It is primal; it is fundamental; it is intrinsically woven into the very fabric of what it means to be a human being. We are born with it.

As previously stated, sound is expressed emotion. As it says in the song above, when you smile you feel better. But singing also taps into and helps release pain and trauma. Consequently, when we prevent ourselves from singing, we prevent ourselves from expressing our profoundest emotions. I categorically state that one cannot access their deepest emotions except through song or chant. Spoken dialogue is simply inadequate. Why?

As I said, the root of the word spirit is spiritus. Spiritus means breath. When we breathe, we are awakening our spiritual selves. When we breathe and connect it to song or chant, we are sustaining spirit and integrating it through a mind/body/spirit paradigm that the spoken word is incapable of accessing.

Singing is so primal that when a newborn nurses, it will often hum. Why? Well, it is naturally nurturing itself and expressing who it is in the most fundamental way possible. It is naturally expressing its joy in the most fundamental way it knows how. Singing is instinctive. It is our natural birthright to sing.

Birthing

The sound of the Self is propelled and sustained by our breath, which becomes a channel for our deepest creativity, as our voice soars out on a magic carpet of air and gives birth to our deepest expression. In that sense, singing is analogous to the experience of giving birth. To illustrate: once at the conclusion of a week-long seminar, I asked everyone to move to a solitary spot in the room and to draw what the experience of finding the voice meant to that individual. Every person, independent of each other, drew something resembling the birth canal.

When we create sound with Vocal Awareness—when we sing—we become cognizant that we are giving birth to who we are. The air pressure, our breath, propels our ideas, our voices, out of our vocal tract and into the world, just as the child is expelled through the pelvic floor and into the world.

The wonderful Lamaze approach to natural childbirth

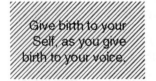

Give birth to your Self, as you give birth to your voice.

teaches exercises to focus a woman at the moment of delivery, so that she is able to release any unnecessary tension in the body that might impede delivery of the child. For example, exercises are taught to release the tension of the inner thighs, which if tightened make releasing the child into the world more difficult. When we sing, more so than when we speak, something similar occurs. That air pressure wells up inside of us, thrusting our voice, our song, out of us— right out of our throats. But if we are tense or frightened, we tighten up; we close down; we make it difficult or impossible to give birth to the inevitable.

Singing—A Cultural Tapestry

Singing has been woven into the path of every culture from the beginning of time. It's portrayed in folk tales and myths.

One of the ways that song is often portrayed is that there are creation hymns, for example, that produce psychic change. There are love producing songs of Iceland and among the Wichita and Micmac Indians. In Ireland, magic power is called down by magic song. There's an Icelandic tale where a person falls on an iceberg and loses a limb, but it is regenerated through the singing of song.

In virtually every culture, at the beginning of creation the gods gave the people song and they were told to use these songs to call the gods back whenever they need at any time. The song will help bring to them things they need, as well as to help transform or banish the things they no longer want. It is in this way that the giving of song is a compassionate act that enables mankind to call forth the gods and the great forces into the human circle.

Song is a special kind of language and the singing of song is a special kind of ability that accomplishes this in a way the spoken voice simply cannot do. Song creates non-ordinary consciousness. It creates a trance state. All humans and many animals, frankly, are susceptible to having consciousness altered by sound.

The great Jungian analyst Clarissa Pinkola Estés, Ph.D., in her groundbreaking book *Women Who Run With the Wolves*, identifies many of these legends about the singing of song and connects them in meaningful ways to our contemporary time and place. She also identifies the singing of song and how the using of the heart in the singing of song awakens layers of the psyche that don't often get breathed or seen. When the spiritus or the breath flow through it opens those apertures—it arouses those previously inaccessible areas of our psyche that we can now begin to access through the use of song.

There is another folk tale about *la-loba*, the Wolf Woman, in Dr. Estés' book. She speaks in the folk tale of *la-loba*, who is an old crag of a woman, who sings and creeps and crawls and sifts through the mountains and arroyos and dry river beds looking for wolf bones and when she has assembled the entire skeleton, she sits by the fire and thinks about what song she will then sing . When she is clear about what she wants to sing, she raises her arms over the skeleton laid before her and sings out—and the animal begins to come to life. The creature is brought fully into being through the singing of song! Then she continues singing even more powerfully and the creature begins to breathe! She sings so deeply that the floor of the desert shakes as she sings and the wolf's eyes open and he leaps up and runs away down the canyon.

When *la-loba* sings over the bones she's gathered she is singing through the use of her "soul-voice," which is to say she's singing on the breath, on her spirit, truths of her own power and her own needs. She breathes her soul over the thing that is ailing and in need of restoration. She descends into the deepest mood of the greatest love, of the greatest feeling . . . her desire for the relationship with her wildest self overflows and she speaks this from her own soul and from that frame of mind. The singing over the bones is an attempt to elicit this great feeling of love from a lover and this woman's labor of finding and singing the creation. *La-loba* is the old one, the one who knows. She is within all of us. She thrives in the deepest soul of all of us, in the ancient and vital parts.

La-loba and the other tales cited here are merely cursory examples of how song is woven into the very sinews—the flesh, bone and marrow of who we are.

Sing Your Heart Out!

The following is excerpted from an article published in Kindermusik Notes magazine, August 1998.

--------------------◆--------------------

. . . I "live, eat, sleep, and breathe" voice! Voice is my passion!

One of the reasons that I'm so thrilled to be involved with Kindermusik is that singing also builds Self-esteem, and because Kindermusik works with children and Kindermusik works with families. It is my belief that when you bring families together through the joy of music, and in this case through the joy of singing, you go a long way in enhancing the family through the unique values that music and singing instill.

Singing is primal. It is a part of the mammalian brain. Singing and speaking developed separately.

Singing is not an outgrowth of the speaking voice. Paleontologists and anthropologists have discovered that when they've gone into caves, for example, in the south of France, to their dismay they find that the caves that have the most profound cave paintings also have the greatest acoustical properties—the point being that there you had people barely above the survival level, not knowing whether they were going to have lunch or whether they were going to be lunch, still finding the need to ritualize chant. It is a part of who we are.

. . . There isn't a people on the face of the earth that doesn't express their profoundest emotions in song or chant. We don't just speak our grief, we wail it. Austere religious groups, such as Shakers and Quakers—why are they called that? Because when they are so filled with the "Spirit of the Lord" that they sing they also shake and quake.

Many years ago there was a task force in my native state, the state of California, entitled the Task Force for Self Esteem and Personal Responsibility. It was developed by one of our congressmen, John Vasconcellos. It was his contention that if you could develop Self-esteem within the tapestry of the society, it would go a long way to helping the society function better. I was invited to be a member of this task force and the project that I documented was "Community Sings"—bringing together people in that old format of the kiosk in the park, having us on the bandstand and just bringing families together for the joy of singing. It might seem kind of an original idea, but let me invite you to go back to a Medieval part book and look at a 12th to 14th century madrigal book and open it up. You will see that the bass line is facing north, the soprano line is facing south, and the alto and tenor lines east and west—because after dinner you'd clear the dishes off, you'd set the songbook in the middle of the table and you'd all then gather around your respective parts and sing. So this is not something new, this community of singing, but it is something we've forgotten how to do.

Kindermusik has recognized the value of music for young families. My work, Vocal Awareness, recognizes the value of voice/song to help us fulfill our covenant with ourselves. Singing is the most hedonistic thing there is to do. The bottom line is that the only reason to do it is it brings me pleasure! When our children come to singing, they don't know they "can't sing" or they're "out of tune." It's we, as adults, who make them feel ill at ease sometimes. Sometimes they may be out of tune, but also sometimes maybe it's our own personal discomfort with singing that makes them uncomfortable. Sometimes, too, perhaps it's that we believe in that old nemesis "tone deafness" (maybe somebody said we were "tone deaf" so we might think the child is "tone deaf"). However, lest there be any doubt, let me not be the first, but hopefully, the last person to tell you that everyone can sing! There is no such thing as "tone deaf."

Another reason I'm so glad to be working with

Kindermusik is that I get to work with you as teachers and you as parents in helping to break down any anxieties or confusions and help bring the most impeccable vocal techniques possible to you so that you have no fear of singing when you're working with your children—that you, too, come to singing as purely, as innocently, and as naturally as the children that you work with do.

I was honored to be a guest last fall in the Washington D.C. area for a Kindermusik symposium and I got to work with Kindermusik teachers from throughout that region. What a joy it was! It was a joy because they really wanted to learn. It was a joy because what brings teachers to Kindermusik in the first place is their love of music. And I got to work with people who were there "for all the right reasons" and we sang children's songs, we sang pop songs, and we truly sang our hearts out. At the end of the day there was not a hoarse voice in the group and in many cases there was not a dry eye in the group—because singing truly reaches into the mind/body/spirit of who we are.

Let me close by giving you a few tips:

1   Remember: singing is joy!
2   Singing helps us resolve personal conflict. Through the lament of "Sometimes I Feel Like A Motherless Child," to the sublimity of "Shenandoah," from the wonderful story of "Whistle a Happy Tune," to the shear spirit of "Zippidee Doo Da," singing puts us in touch with

our true essences.

3 Singing is simple. So remember the K.I.S.S. approach: Keep It Simple Sweetheart.

4 Employing my copyrighted Vocal Awareness method, experience the difference between "taking a breath" and "allowing a silent and loving down through your body breath."

5 Always sing in "stature." (Feel what your body does when you stand or sit in stature. Notice how it breathes, how it lifts up, how it releases tension.)

6 Discover the difference between "dropping your jaw" and releasing your jaw. I'd rather have you release your jaw. In addition to this thought I want you to also release your tongue, your neck and your shoulders whenever you're singing.

7 All tension is fear-based, so why sing with fear?

8 Support. Feel the difference between pulling your stomach in and pulling your stomach up and in. In Vocal Awareness support means to "pull your stomach up and through the sound."

9 Have a wonderful time!

10 Sing and teach from conscious awareness. Quoting Frank Sinatra, "From the minute you step into that spotlight you've got to know exactly what you're doing every second on that stage, otherwise it's all goodnight."

11 Thank your Source. Begin your singing, practicing, teaching with a simple "thank you to the Source."

12 (I guess we'll call this the "12 step program".) Be My Self. Don't present when you teach or share with

your children, just be. Don't feel self-conscious—*if* singing is challenging, just be conscious of Self and allow yourself to truly reveal who you are. Enjoy the discovery.

In closing, I want to say thank you for the opportunity to be a part of Kindermusik. I am yours in song.

Singing with Vocal Awareness

I have a student who has the potential to become a world-class opera singer. She came through the "head/chest" school of voice, a standard approach to operatic training that is so often taught in a regimented, compartmentalized and extremely uncreative way, and had many years of technical and academic study. When she first came to see me, however, she was as far from achieving her full potential as if she were still a beginner. Although her vocal instrument was spectacular, she exhibited extraordinary fear when she sang. This fear significantly inhibited her singing and left her completely disconnected from the beauty of her voice and from the ease and joy of singing.

One day we were exploring the principle of "paying attention," attempting to remove the block to her vocal expression, and in our discussion we were distinguishing between the fear of failure and the fear of success. She recalled being a child in a convent school in Peru, being a joyful child filled with the spirit of song. She loved to sing and was always the lead singer in choirs and performances. Yet the sisters would also criticize her, saying, "You talk too much."

As our conversation continued, we discovered that she was unconsciously afraid to let herself sing fully and beautifully because she was afraid the sisters of her childhood would again chastise her. We also discovered that when she abandoned herself to the song and her singing, she felt as if she were experiencing the breath of God coming through her—a feeling that seemed blasphemous to her. "How dare I be allowed to have such an experience?" she exclaimed. "How dare you not?" I replied. Like so many of us she had shut down her voice and was left with the torture, pain and paralysis that shutting down brings. Now she understood that if she were to sing to her fullest potential, she would have to change her consciousness and recapture what she had naturally as a child.

Some time later this beautiful woman and her husband produced her first album and a concert—a magnificent evening of tango music filled with power and passion. She was stupendous! Fully conscious and in charge of her destiny—no fear, no excuses. Through her focus and newly found ability to pay attention deeply, this lovely woman had taken the journey inward and had learned how to create a new version of herself—a version she had chosen.

As her experience demonstrates, Vocal Awareness is as much a training for the professional singer as for the non-professional. And the would-be professional has the option to choose or not to choose—one of the basic Vocal Awareness axioms—to sing or not to sing, to be or not be a professional singer.

The perfect example of someone who made his own choices is Joe Namath, the former great American football player. Joe studied with me for many years. Initially, his only motivation for studying was simply because he wanted to sing. And so we worked on it. But it was a real challenge for Joe to learn to sing on pitch.

After many months, he performed on a television show and sang just a little bit. He decided he wanted to do a musical. The first musical we worked on together was *Li'l Abner*. Joe practiced hard, but his pitch was never quite dependable. At the first show in Atlanta, in a 2,000-seat theater, Joe still wasn't firmly in touch with how to stay on pitch. In fact, at one point, he was so out of tune that when he finally got back on pitch the audience burst into applause.

But Joe was very much his own man. He had chosen what he wanted to do, and he kept doing it. And he kept growing and improving. He improved to the point that several years later, when he performed in a musical called *Sugar* at the Dorothy Chandler Pavilion in Los Angeles, his singing was quite wonderful—very Rex Harrisonesque—with a nice baritone quality and, honestly, always on pitch.

Another colorful example of someone who chose to sing and learned through Vocal Awareness is Sylvester Stallone. Sylvester studied singing with me in preparation for a picture he was doing. We began to vocalize during the first couple of lessons and he did quite well. In fact, it turned out that Sylvester liked to sing but had never formally studied. Then during one lesson, his brother, Frank Stallone, came in. Frank has been a popular singer. When he left, Sylvester began to sing again but did not do as well as he had done before his brother had come in. He was tense and a little off pitch, because his brother had come in and at some level this had caused some conflict for Sylvester.

A few weeks later, Frank again came by while Sylvester and I were working. Sylvester invited him in and said, "Hey, Frankie, let's see who can hold his notes the longest. Let's see how high we can sing together." Nothing stopped Sylvester.

I consider Sylvester a wonderful rock-and-roll singer. He loves the joy of singing. The point of this story is simply that you don't need to let anything stop you if that is what you truly want to do. You simply have to choose it and pursue it with total dedication and without judgement.

I have mentioned often in this book the necessity to work without judgement. Frederica von Stade, who has carved out for herself an extraordinary and unique career as an operatic and theatrical performer, in an interview in *The New York Times* (November 12, 1995: H35) was quoted as saying:

◆

I've never liked my voice. I can't stand it. I think it's because I hear all the imperfections, but I get up every morning and face it because it's my means of expression, and I love that. And I love the physical sensation of singing . . . the voice renders you eternally humble. It's so unpredictable and fragile and so different through your different passages of life.

Singing is for Everyone

Give yourself permission to sing. Join a local church or community choir. Many non-professional singers begin their career in the local choir and continue in choirs after they become professional. Many other non-professional singers find their fulfillment singing in the shower. *Singing is for everyone.*

Anyone can sing! Sing around the house. Sing with your children. Have you ever seen an inhibited three-year-old? It's virtually an oxymoron. Are three-year-olds afraid to sing? No, of course not. Singing is so natural.

As in all the other chapters in this book, I am trying to take you back to your natural birthright—to help you unlearn, relearn and reconnect to what was naturally yours before you gave it away. Let us reacquire that Self. What better place to start than with the joy of singing!

So again, to address the question, "Why sing?"—I think, frankly, the question should be, "Why not?"

CHAPTER 13

Vocal Awareness: Creating a New Mythology

Welcome to the end and to the beginning. I hope that the journey you've taken to bring you to this point has been illuminating and rewarding. As you now know, Vocal Awareness recognizes that the journey outward is always and only the journey inward. And by now you know what the metaphor means. As you do this work on a regular basis, remember that the only reason for doing it is to bring you joy, sovereignty—and personal empowerment.

Remember my mission statement where I say, "I want to help all the people I work with to achieve their own enlightenment and enjoy their own empowerment." Vocal

Awareness and the dissemination of its principles is my vocation, my calling, my lifelong artistic and professional passion. Why do I tell you this? Not because I think Vocal Awareness will be as central to your life as it is to mine, but because I would like you to see Vocal Awareness as being as fundamental to your life as breathing and communicating are. I would hope that its principles would be integrated into your mission and support you in your own life journey.

The practice of Vocal Awareness can be a bulwark against the changing tides of life. It offers a metaphorical, spiritual and practical structure upon which, in *your* way and through *your* power, you can build a life of honor and success. I want in these closing words to inspire you, but also to remind you to always do the work as specifically as possible. Please do not assume that because you have come this far on your journey, you have mastered Vocal Awareness. Rather, having come this far, I am sure you recognize that you are just beginning your journey. But to regard this beginning as the onset of an arduous trek with increasingly brutal challenges is not what I want for you either. Instead, I want you to see this as the beginning of a new phase of your life. I hope that as you close the last page of this book, you will see yourself as embarking upon the most exhilarating chapter of your new life, and that you will view Vocal Awareness as a trusted and dear friend—one that has brought you closer to your Self, made you a better listener to yourself and others, and made you one who no longer judges. I hope it has supported you and helped you learn how always to represent yourself from the gestalt of who you are, from the wholeness of who you are.

I so love living a life guided by and supported with the conscious awareness that Vocal Awareness shows me. I merely have to require myself to surrender to its ethic because Vocal Awareness has taught me so well how to be the best of myself possible at all times. I long ago recognized that there are no shortcuts, that, in fact, *the only way out is through.*

So, my friend (and I hope by this time you feel as though we have become friends, because through these pages we have both shared a lot), complete the book and then put it aside. When necessary, return to it as needed, as you would return to a quiet corner for solace, or to a dear teacher for inspiration and guidance. Continue your ascent. Continue soaring. *Feel the full investiture of your Self in every breath, in every sound and with the fullest integration of mind/body/spirit.*

Thank you for your trust. Thank you for sharing yourself.

Personal Helicon

As a child, they could not keep me from wells
and old pumps with buckets and windlasses.
I loved the dark drop, the trapped sky, the smells
Of waterweed, fungus and dank moss.

One, in a brickyard, with a rotted board top.
I savoured the rich crash when a bucket
Plummeted down at the end of a rope.
So deep you saw no reflection in it.

A shallow one under a dry stone ditch
Fructified like any aquarium.
When you dragged out long roots from the soft mulch
A white face hovered over the bottom.
Others had echoes, gave back your own call
With a clean new music in it. And one
Was scaresome for there, out of the ferns and tall
Foxgloves, a rat slapped across my reflection.

Now, to pry into roots, to finger slime,
to stare, big-eyed Narcissus, into some spring
Is beneath all adult dignity. I rhyme
To see myself. To set the darkness echoing.

Seamus Heaney

Sources

"Acoustics of the Singing Voice." *Scientific American* (March 1977).

Arnheim, Rudolf. *Visual Thinking*. London: Faber & Faber, 1969.

Bly, Robert. *Iron John: A Book About Men*. Reading, Mass.: Addison-Wesley, 1990.

Campbell, Joseph. *The Power of Myth*. New York: Vintage Books, 1955.

Chatwin, Bruce. *The Songlines*. New York: Penguin, 1987.

Chavannes, Edouard. *The Historical Memoirs of Su-Ma-Tsien* (or Chou Ma Tchien). Translated from the French by Dane Rudhyar.

Chopra, Deepak, M.D. *Ageless Body, Timeless Mind*. New York: Harmony Books, 1993.

Cousins, Norman. *Anatomy of an Illness*. New York: Norton, 1979.

Gibran, Kahlil. *Secrets of the Heart.* Secaucus, N.J.: Citadel Press, 1978.

Hamilton, Edith. *The Greek Way.* New York: Norton, 1942.

Hawking, Stephen. *A Brief History of Time: From the Big Bang to Black Holes.* New York: Bantam Books, 1988.

Herrigel, Eugen. *Zen in the Art of Archery.* New York: Vintage Books, 1989.

Hesse, Hermann. *Siddhartha.* London: Peter Owen, 1954.

Hofstadter, Douglas R. *Godel, Escher, Bach: An Eternal Golden Braid.* New York: Vintage Books, 1920.

Hunt, Valerie V. *Infinite Mind: The Science of Human Vibration.* Malibu, Calif.: Malibu Publishing, 1995.

Joy, Brugh, M.D. *Joy's Way.* Los Angeles: J.P. Tarcher, 1979.

Kierkegaard, Soren. *Fear and Trembling.* Princeton, N.J.: Princeton University Press, 1983.

Lilly, John C, M.D. *Communication Between Man and Dolphin.* New York: Crown, 1978.

Lundin, Robert W. *An Objective Psychology of Music.* New York: John Wiley, 1967.

Miller, Richard. *The Structure of Singing.* New York: Schirmer Books, 1996.

Moyers, Bill. *Healing and the Mind.* New York: Doubleday, 1995.

National Association of Teachers of Singing. Monthly magazine with articles on singing and voice research. Publication office: 2800 University Blvd. N., JU Station, Jacksonville, FL 32211.

Nettl, Bruno. *Folk and Traditional Music of the Western Continents.* New York: Prentice-Hall, 1965.

Pearce, Joseph Chilton. *Magical Child: Rediscovering Nature's Plan for Our Children*. New York: Dutton, 1977.

Pinkola Estés, Clarissa, Ph.D. *Women Who Run With the Wolves: Myths and Stories of the Wild Woman Archetype*. (New York: Ballantine Publishing Group, 1992).

Pleasants, Henry. *The Great Singers: From the Dawn of Opera to Our Own Time*. New York: Simon and Schuster, 1966.

Rudhyar, Dane. *The Magic of Tone and the Art of Music*. Boulder, Colo.: Shambhala, 1982.

Sartre, Jean Paul. *Nausea*. Cambridge, Mass.: R. Bentley, 1964.

Schafer, R. Murray. *The Tuning of the World*. New York: Knopf, 1977.

Shankkar, Ravi. *My Music—My Life*. New York: Simon & Schuster, 1968.

Smith, W.J. *A Dictionary of Musical Terms in Four Languages*. London: Hutchinson and Co., 1961. (The languages are English, French, Italian and German.)

Smolover, Raymond. *The Vocal Essence*. Covenant Publications, 1971.

Tomatis, Alfred A. *The Conscious Ear*. Barrytown, N.Y.: Station Hill Press, 1991.

Ulrich, Homer. *Music: A Design for Listening*. New York: Harcourt, Brace & World, 1962.

Vennard, William. *Singing: The Mechanism and the Technique*. New York: Carl Fischer, 1967.

Weitz, Morris. *Problems in Aesthetics*. New York: Macmillan, 1963.

About the Author

A rthur Samuel Joseph is a voice specialist in private practice in Encino, California. He is the creator of *Vocal Awareness* and has been teaching and lecturing for over three decades throughout the United States, Europe, Japan and Mexico.

He has been on the faculty of the University of Southern California and has taught Master classes at Yale University, George Washington University and the Esalen Institute in Big Sur, California.

Mr. Joseph holds a Master of Arts in Music with an emphasis on German *Lieder,* which he studied with Martial Singher at the Music Academy of the West, Montecito, California. Mr. Joseph has also studied extensively in the areas of philosophy and psychology. He earned memberships in the performing unions—American Federation of Television and Radio Artists, as well as Actors Equity—at age 18. Mr. Joseph still performs regularly.

In 1979, Mr. Joseph was elected a member of the National Association of Teachers of Singing, Inc. and in 1980 was invited to conduct vocal research at the Institute for the Advanced Studies of the Communication Processes at the University of Florida.

Mr. Joseph has lectured internationally. In England for the Association of Teachers of Singing; in France for the International Congress of Voice Teachers; in Austria for the Tanz Gesang Studio at the National Theatre; in Japan for the Japan Association of Research on Singing; in the United States and Canada for the Learning Annex, among others.

Mr. Joseph has a highly successful five-tape, audio/ workbook series that includes ten songs with accompaniment, published by Sounds True Audio.

Mr. Joseph has devoted his artistic and professional life to Vocal Awareness and to serving his mission statement, which in part states that he wants to "help all those he works with to achieve their own enlightenment and enjoy their own empowerment."

He applies his original principles of mind/body/spirit integration through voice in all walks of life, from boardrooms to the Broadway stage, rock-and-roll to opera, the classroom to the living room. He teaches toddlers and senior adults; one-on-one private sessions and public forums of 1,000, and his work has been translated from English to Spanish, French, German, Japanese, Italian and other languages. Vocal Awareness has been taught successfully to people from all walks of life.

For further information on Arthur Joseph or Vocal Awareness, please contact:

The Vocal Awareness Institute
P.O. Box 261021
Encino, CA 91426-1021

e-mail: Vawareness@aol.com

Visit our website at http://www.vocalawareness.com.